Augustin Joseph Louage

A course of philosophy

Embracing logic, metaphysics and ethics

Augustin Joseph Louage

A course of philosophy
Embracing logic, metaphysics and ethics

ISBN/EAN: 9783741196324

Manufactured in Europe, USA, Canada, Australia, Japa

Cover: Foto ©Klaus-Uwe Gerhardt /pixelio.de

Manufactured and distributed by brebook publishing software (www.brebook.com)

Augustin Joseph Louage

A course of philosophy

PREFACE.

IT is the unanimous opinion of those best qualified to judge, that a knowledge of the first principles of Philosophy is necessary to complete any course of classical or scientific studies. Experience as well as reason teaches that those who complete their education with a course of sound Philosophy, thus acquire an accurate method for the continuation of their studies, for the instruction of others, or for the pursuit of any calling to which they may devote their talents.

The man who learns what truth is, learns also to love it; and will not be easily led astray by the systems of error which are everywhere paraded before him, labelled with the false appellation of Philosophy: he despises the contradictions of pseudo-philosophers, he abhors the repulsive doctrines of the wicked, and avoids with care the corruption of morals which always accompanies them. Everywhere and always he perceives the presence of the Divinity, and is accordingly filled with awe and reverence: he sees also, with consolation, the excellence of his own soul and its future destiny, and not only preserves it from the contamination of vice, but also adorns it with every virtue; thus conscientiously discharging all the duties of his station in life, he must ascend higher and higher in the scale of being.

When we thus point out the abundant and inestimable fruits of Philosophy, it is evident that we do not speak of that so-called Philosophy which ignores the light of Divine revelation, but of that true Christian Philosophy which is guided as far as possible by reason, but which freely admits the light of faith where that of reason fails: for, as we shall see, reason alone is not capable of completely solving some of the most serious problems which concern the salvation of man.

The young man who, while at college, has either wholly neglected to study the rules of judging and knowing, or who has not engraven them deeply on his mind, wanders without a guide through dark and devious ways, and is "carried about by every wind of doctrine." He reads indiscriminately every book, good or bad, that chance throws in his way, and peruses them with little attention or reflection. Hence he fills his mind with imperfect notions of things, without any order; everywhere he sees contradictory systems, and in the midst of this general darkness he remains uncertain of the truth, and even becomes doubtful of the very existence of certitude. Soon the truth of religion appears to him as not sufficiently proved; and, owing to the prejudices to which he has yielded, he begins to deny that there is any excellence in virtue or any turpitude in vice. Passions rise in his heart, which, not being restrained, but rather flattered and excited by many causes, soon lead to deplorable results; for they shake his reason, which is already weak and deprived of its natural support, they destroy the vigor of his physical system, they deprave his nature, and finally carry the unfortunate youth to utter destruction.

That this is not an overdrawn picture is plain to any one who chooses to look around him with an unprejudiced eye; and it shows conclusively the importance of a knowledge of the primary principles of Philosophy. On this knowledge, in truth, depends the progress which we shall make in science, the solidity of our mind, our love of truth and detestation of falsehood, our sagacity in choosing what is best, the integrity of our morals, the peace of families, the well-being of society, in a word, our happiness both in public and in private life.

The teacher, therefore, who is incompetent, negligent or dishonest, is the cause of an irreparable loss to those under his care; while he who is learned, diligent and consistent in his instruction, sows in the minds of those committed to his charge the seeds of truth and virtue which will bring forth an abundant harvest of the richest fruits of a good education. To attain so desirable an end, the pupil should be guided, not by obscure and uncertain precepts, but by those which are established upon the clearest principles of reason: even as a child as yet unacquainted with the way is guided, not by the hand of an ignorant or a dangerous man, but by that of his father.

We do not approve of the method of teaching Philosophy by lecture; for long lectures, however well developed, are not always understood by the student and are very easily forgotten: we are rather in favor of placing in the hands of the pupil a small but comprehensive text-book, which he can readily commit to memory, and easily retain. Such a text-book should be concise without being obscure, so that the attention of the student may be sufficiently attracted and exercised; but, more than all, a book written for this object should be exact.

An elementary book of this kind is not often found; indeed it may be doubted whether one possessing all the qualities mentioned above exists in any modern tongue. Some excellent compendiums written in the Latin language have been published since 1825; but they cannot serve our purpose, which requires a manual of Philosophy adapted particularly to the wants of those who are not acquainted with the classics. To unlock the treasures of Philosophy for them, we concluded that it would be well to prepare a text-book having as far as possible the requisites mentioned above.

During the preparation of our manual we have diligently consulted the best works on the subject; and we now submit the result of our labors in the form of an elementary text-book on Philosophy, which we trust will meet the requirements of those for whom it is intended: and may God grant that, owing to the good intentions of the author, this book may be the means of advancing the best interests of the youths for whom it was written.

S. N. D. B.

INTRODUCTORY.

BEFORE entering the sanctuary of Philosophy, a few words are necessary by way of introduction. We shall arrange these preliminary remarks under four heads. Under the *first* we shall give the DEFINITIONS of several WORDS of common occurrence: under the *second* we shall examine the DEFINITIONS of PHILOSOPHY: under the *third* we shall give the DIVISIONS OF PHILOSOPHY: and under the *fourth* we shall say something of ARGUMENT.

I.
DEFINITIONS OF WORDS.

A BEING or THING is that which *exists* or *may exist:* it is therefore twofold, real or possible.

EXISTENCE is the *real union* of the parts or attributes which constitute a being.

POSSIBILITY is the *agreement* of the attributes which constitute a being, in such a way that its existence does not involve any contradiction.

The ATTRIBUTES are the *qualities* of a being: they are *essential* or *constitutive* when the thing cannot exist without them, and *accidental* when the thing can exist without them.

The ESSENCE of a being consists of the collection of

its essential or *necessary* attributes. The essence of a thing is also called its *nature;* although the word *nature* is more extensive than *essence*, since the nature of a being sometimes includes its accidental as well as its essential attributes. *Nature* is also used to signify the whole collection of corporeal beings.

A GENUS is a collection of beings having one or more attributes common to each. A genus must be sufficiently general to be divided into subordinate classes, called *species*.

A SPECIES, therefore, is a collection of beings belonging to one and the same genus, but having particular and constitutive properties by which they are distinguished from any other collection of beings of the same genus.

For example, *being*, the most general genus, is divided into two species, *corporeal* and *incorporeal* beings. These two species are each divided into other species, and consequently they are genera with reference to the subsequent divisions. Corporeal bodies form two species, things *with life* and things *without life*. Things with life, considered with reference to a further division, form a genus which is divided into two species, *animals* and *vegetables*.

The genus may be either *remote* or *proximate*. It is remote when there is at least one division intervening between the species and the genus referred to. For instance, when I say, *Man* is a rational *being*, the genus, *being*, is remote; but it is proximate when I say, *Man* is a rational *animal*.

Each species must have an *essential attribute* which makes it distinct from every other species of the same genus: this attribute is called the DIFFERENCE. When this difference consists of an attribute which separates every being of the species from every being of another species, it is called the SPECIFIC DIFFERENCE. We have an example of this difference in the following definition, Man is a rational animal, where the word *rational* indicates the specific difference, distinguishing man from any other species of the genus animal.

INDIVIDUALS are those beings to which, considered separately, the *same genus* and the *same difference* pertain.

In *Ontology* we shall give the definitions of *Substance, Modification, Subject* and *Object*, also of *Order* and *Relation*.

SCIENCE is a series of notions deduced from principles firmly established, disposed in a methodical order and referring to one and the same object.

Science is either *subjective* or *objective;* subjective when we consider it as existing in our own minds, and objective when we consider it as existing in the object contemplated: it is again either *speculative* or *practical.*

Practical science is the source of *art.*

ART is the application of science to external things, according to determined rules. We will here observe that the same species of knowledge may be at the same time a science and an art. Arithmetic and Geometry, considered in themselves, are sciences; but applied to external things they are arts. Logic, considered in itself, is a science; but applied to the investigation of truth and its manifestation, according to determined rules, as in the method of Aristotle, it is the Art of Reasoning, or the Art of Thinking.

KNOWLEDGE, in general, is the representation taking place in the mind, of something, in some manner; it differs very little from *idea*, as we shall see. It is *intuitive* when the object appears so clearly to our intellect that we perceive it without reasoning, and *discursive* when we need some demonstration to perceive the object.

Knowledge has for its objects either natural or supernatural things.

FAITH, in general, is the assent of the mind to some truth, on the testimony of another person. When this assent is founded upon the authority of God, it is Divine Faith; it is Human Faith when established upon the testimony of men.

II.

DEFINITIONS OF PHILOSOPHY.

It often becomes necessary to give *definitions*, in order to avoid obscurity or uncertainty. A DEFINITION is an explanation of a *word* or of a *thing*. The definition of a word is said to be *etymological* when its origin is given, and *significative* when its meaning is explained.

The definition of a thing is that which shows the nature of the thing. It may be merely descriptive, and then the definition is called *imperfect;* or it may be *accurate* and *perfect*, and this only deserves the name of definition. Description is suitable to oratory, but definition belongs especially to Philosophy: it gives precisely what is necessary in order that the thing may be understood and distinguished from every other thing, by enumerating its essential qualities.

Three conditions are requisite to a perfect definition: 1st, It must be *clear*, that is, free from any obscure or ambiguous expression; 2nd, It must be *brief*, that is, free from all unnecessary words; and 3d, It must give the *proximate genus* and the *specific difference*. When these three conditions are found, the definition applies to the thing defined, and to nothing else, so that the thing and its definition are reciprocals.

PHILOSOPHY has been defined as "the science of things knowable by the light of reason," or "the science of reason."

But these definitions, while they distinguish Philosophy from theology, do not separate it from the physical and mathematical sciences; and in our day these sciences have been so far extended that they have ceased to belong to Philosophy, as it is now taught in the schools. The following definition of Philosophy might consequently be accepted: "The science of supersensible things knowable by the light of reason." This definition has the three requisite marks: it is *clear*, *short*, and contains the *proximate genus*, "science," and the *specific difference*, "supersensible," which word distinguishes Philosophy from the physical sciences, and "knowable by the light of reason," which words distinguish Philosophy from theology.

III.
Divisions of Philosophy.

Division, in general, is the distribution of a whole into its parts. A WHOLE is that which is formed of parts really or logically distinct. The whole is said to be *metaphysical, physical* or *logical*, according as its parts belong to one or other of these orders.

The division, to be accurate, must have these three conditions: 1st, It must be *adequate*, that is, it must include as many members as there are in the whole which is to be divided; 2nd, It must be *distinct*, that is, one part must not be included in another; 3d, The parts must be *proximate*, otherwise there would be confusion, the following division, for instance, would be wrong: Living beings are divided into three classes, men, beasts and plants. A proximate division would be: Living beings are divided into two classes, animals and vegetables, and so continue, always giving first the proximate, or nearest, division, and the subdivisions in like order.

Philosophy, as we have learned, is the science of supersensible things. In order to proceed methodically in the acquisition of this science, we must first give the rules for the investigation of truth, and then investigate the things which form the object of this science, beginning with the most important, namely, God and the soul. The nature of God and the soul being known, we may examine the relations existing between God and the soul, between the soul and the body, and finally the relations of men to each other considered as social beings. We have then three parts which form the DIVISIONS OF PHILOSOPHY: namely, *Logic*, *Metaphysics*, and *Ethics*.

IV.

ARGUMENT.

The different points to be treated under this head will be given in *Logic*. We will here say only a few words in regard to equivocal propositions, which we may sometimes have to deal with.

1st. We must distinguish and point out clearly the equivocal expressions.

2nd. If these expressions are not clear of themselves, we must define and explain them.

3d. We must concede the proposition in the sense in which it is true, and deny it in the sense in which it is false; and in both cases give our reasons for doing so, if necessary.

A COURSE OF PHILOSOPHY.

PART I.—LOGIC.

LOGIC.

Definition—Division.

FOR the acquisition of science the human mind must first be provided with rules, and so be enabled to avoid error and establish truth on the solid foundation of reason.

The word philosophy, as we have seen, is as universal as the word science itself, and logic is the key of this science. Logic is consequently the first part of Philosophy, the part which treats of the first efforts of the human mind to discover truth, and afterwards gives rules by which this truth may be demonstrated. We may therefore define Logic to be, "The science which directs the operations of our mind in the investigation and demonstration of truth."

When this science is put in practice it becomes "The Art of Reasoning," which words may be accepted as a definition of logic, considered as an art.

In the foregoing definitions we find the three requisite conditions of a good definition: 1st, clearness, 2nd, conciseness, and 3d, reciprocity, that is, the proximate genus and the specific difference are given.

The natural order observed by the mind in the investigation of truth may be described as follows: We first represent objects to ourselves, we next judge of them, we then compare our judgments and draw conclusions, and, finally, we arrange these conclusions in a certain order. Hence we have in the science of logic four different parts or divisions; the first treating of our Ideas of objects, the second of our Judgments concerning those ideas, the third of our Reasoning concerning the judgments, and the fourth of the Method in which we dispose of the conclusions of our reasoning.

As soon as we have considered these four divisions of the science we shall apply it to the investigation of the existence of truth, or Certitude; and, logically speaking, this question comes first. Is there anything certain, is there any certitude? and, if so, how can we prove its existence? Although this question, in reality, forms the introduction to the study of Philosophy, since without an affirmative answer to it we cannot make one step in the science, yet some authors treat it as a part of logic; and we adopt this plan as more convenient, and shall therefore treat of certitude as the fifth part of logic.

FIRST DISSERTATION.

ON IDEAS.

An idea may be considered as existing either in the mind or out of it: consequently this first dissertation may be divided into two chapters.

CHAPTER FIRST.

OF IDEAS CONSIDERED AS EXISTING IN THE MIND.

"An idea is the mere representation in the mind of some object." We cannot, therefore, have an idea of *nothing;* for *nothing* has no property or attribute by which it might be represented in the mind. The definition of an idea being given, we have now to examine, 1st, the division of ideas, 2nd, their properties, and 3d, the operations of our mind in regard to them.

§I. THE DIVISION OF IDEAS.

In regard to their *origin*, some authors divide ideas into three classes: First, *innate* ideas, or those born with us; second, *adventitious* ideas, or those coming to us from various causes in the course of time; and third, *factitious* ideas, or those formed by ourselves.

In regard to their *object*, we have, first, the idea of *substance*, when we consider the substance of a thing as abstracted from its modifications; second, the idea of *modification*, when we consider the modifications of a thing as abstracted from its substance (these two ideas are called *abstract* ideas); and, third, the idea of *modified substance*, which is called a *concrete* idea.

Concrete ideas may be produced by sensation or by the imagination. They are produced by sensation when they represent objects which strike our senses and which, therefore, really exist: they are produced by the imagination when they represent objects which may exist, but which do not strike our senses.

All these ideas are called ideas of sensible things when their objects are sensible things; and they are called ideas of intellectual things when the objects which they represent cannot affect the senses: the ideas of moral things belong to this second class.

An idea is *simple* when the object represented cannot be divided, as, "an affirmation;" *complex* when the object is qualified, as, "a good man;" *compound* when the object may be divided into several parts, as, "a horse," "a tree;" *collective*, when the object is a unity formed of several objects belonging to the same species, as, "an army;" *universal* when the object represents all the beings of the same species, as, "man in general;" *particular* when the object represents only a part of the beings belonging to the same species, as, "several men;" *singular* when the object refers to one individual of a collection, as, "Peter," "John;" and *adequate* when the object appears with all its attributes: God only has adequate ideas, we have but inadequate ones.

§ II. Properties of Ideas.

Ideas are, first, either *true* or *false*. They are true when they conform with their objects, false when they do not. But since this conformity is always with the objects as represented in our minds, and not as they may be in reality, we may, with this explanation, admit the opinion of those who pretend that there are no false ideas. Ideas are, in the second place, either *clear* or *obscure*, and these words need no explanation. Thirdly, they are either *distinct* or *confused*. An idea is distinct when it can be readily separated from any other idea, as the idea of "a certain *house*" or of "a certain *person;*" and it is confused when the object cannot be distinctly determined. If I say, "Many *persons* are standing at a distance from me, and I cannot see whether they are armed or not," I have a confused idea.

The *comprehension* of an idea signifies the sum of the attributes which constitute the nature of the object. The comprehension of the idea of man includes everything necessary to constitute a man, as man, thus distinguishing him from everything else, as a tree or a stone.

The *extension* of an idea signifies the whole collection of the individuals which the same idea embraces. The extension of the idea of man includes all those beings that have the human nature, that is, all men.

§ III. OPERATIONS OF THE MIND IN REGARD TO IDEAS.

The principal operations of the mind in reference to ideas are attention, abstraction and comparison.

Attention is that operation of the mind by which we lay our ideas, as it were, before the eyes of the mind, in order to examine them with care and master them. Attention and reflection constitute the foundation of science and the source of learning.

Abstraction is that operation of the mind by which we consider one or more qualities of an object, the other qualities being laid aside. Abstraction is not only possible and even easy of attainment, but it is also necessary.

Having examined several qualities and found that they belong to a certain object, if we unite these qualities in order to form this object again, we perform an operation which is called *synthesis:* on the contrary, if an object is given us to study, and we divide it into its parts, examining successively each part, we perform an operation which is called *analysis*. We may, therefore, see that analysis is a decomposition, while synthesis is a recomposition.

When, in order to form a species, we collect several individuals having Common properties, we perform an operation which is called *generalization*.

When we consider two or more ideas, in order to find their consistency or their inconsistency, we perform an operation which is called *comparison*. This operation is, of course, the most important; without it we could not improve in any branch of science or art.

CHAPTER SECOND.

Of Ideas Considered as Existing Out of the Mind.

There are three ways by which we may express what we represent to our mind, namely, gestures, speech and writing; and these three are designated by the general appellation of *signs*.

For the development of this chapter see the remarks on the "Origin of Language," in experimental Psychology.

SECOND DISSERTATION.

ON JUDGMENT.

When the mind after having compared two ideas declares their consistency or their inconsistency, it makes a *judgment*. Consequently "Judgment is that operation of the mind by which it pronounces on the consistency or the inconsistency of two ideas, or declaring that a certain quality exists or does not exist in a certain object. We may readily understand that our errors proceed from mistaken judgments only, for we cannot err in perceiving or in feeling.

Here again we may consider judgment as existing either in the mind or out of it, and consequently this dissertation is also divided into two chapters.

CHAPTER FIRST.

OF JUDGMENT CONSIDERED AS EXISTING IN THE MIND.

Judgment is a positive act of the mind, and not a mere sensation, as Condillac said, or a perception, according to the opinion of Mallebranche. It is an act, since we judge and pronounce, and we can do neither without acting; it is, besides, a simple act, since it consists of an affirmation or a negation, and, consequently, cannot be divided.

Judgment is very probably produced both by the intellect and by the will.

A judgment is either *necessary* or *free*. A necessary judgment is one formed when the mind is so strongly impelled to judge that it cannot refrain from judging. "I exist," is a necessary judgment.

A free judgment is one which the mind is not forced to pronounce.

A judgment is, in the second place, either *true* or *false*, depending on the fact as to whether the things are, or are not, as the mind declares them to be.

Thirdly, a judgment is *certain* when it is established on an infallible foundation, as, "Our Lord died," "Bodies exist."

Fourthly, a judgment is *evident* when it rests upon a clear and distinct perception of the consistency or the inconsistency of two ideas, as, "Two and two equal four."

Lastly, a *probable* judgment is one established on trustworthy, but not infallible, reasons, as, "It is probable that a sick man will recover when several good physicians are of opinion that such will be the case."

CHAPTER SECOND.

Of Judgment Considered as Existing out of the Mind.

When we express our judgment we form what is called a *proposition*. To constitute a proposition three terms are necessary, a *subject*, a *verb*, and an *attribute*, one or even two of which may be understood.

In every proposition the attribute always expresses a notion more extensive than the subject. Aristotle gives ten classifications of attributes, which he calls *de categoriis;* Kant gives but four. Nothing is more obscure and less useful than such classifications.

A proposition is *universal* when the subject is taken

in all its extension, as, "Every substance is divisible," "No spirit is mortal."

A proposition is *particular* when the subject is not taken in its full extension, as, "Some men are learned." Even such expressions as "All young men are fickle" are but particular propositions.

A proposition is *singular* when the subject is but one individual, as, "Cæsar was a great general."

A proposition is *affirmative* when the attribute is declared to be consistent with the subject, *negative* when declared inconsistent.

The following axioms in reference to affirmative and negative propositions are given in this connection; we shall need them farther on:

1st Axiom. The attribute of an affirmative proposition is taken in its entire comprehension, but not in its entire extension; consequently, the attribute of an affirmative proposition is a particular term. For example, if I say "All angels are spirits," the attribute "spirits" is taken in its entire comprehension, but not in its entire extension; for other beings than angels may be spirits.

2d Axiom. The attribute of a negative proposition is not taken in its entire comprehension, but is taken in its entire extension; consequently, the attribute of a negative proposition is a universal term. For example, if I say, "A man is not a stone," the attribute "stone" is not taken in its entire comprehension, since both "man" and "stone" have the comprehension of material substance; but it is taken in its whole extension, for no stone whatever is a man.

A proposition is *grammatical* when we consider

only the terms as abstracted from the sense, and *logical* when we consider the proposition as having a determined sense.

The sense of a logical proposition may be *proper* or *foreign:* it is proper, or natural, when we give to the words their ordinary meaning; and it is foreign when we give to the terms a signification which is not their own.

The sense may also be either *divided* or *composite;* or, to use the Latin expressions, the proposition may be taken either in *sensu diviso* or in *sensu composito.* For instance, if I say, "The blind may see," the proposition is true in *sensu diviso,* but false in *sensu composito.* In the first sense the proposition means, "The blind, if restored to sight, may see;" in the second it means, "The blind, though remaining blind, may see." In the course of this work we shall have more to say of this distinction.

A proposition is *true* when it declares its subject to be as it is in reality, as, "God is powerful;" and *false* when it declares its subject to be as it is not in reality, as, "God is cruel."

Sometimes a proposition has two senses, and then it is called *equivocal.* To obtain the true sense of a proposition it is often necessary to stake the proposition in a different manner, to change the order in which the terms have been first presented; sometimes also when two propositions are given and compared it becomes necessary to judge of the contrary or the contradictory of one of them: it is therefore necessary for us to learn something of the conversion and the opposition of propositions.

§I. Conversion of Propositions.

The *conversion* of a proposition is the changing of it into another proposition of the same meaning.

This conversion is *simple* when the whole attribute is substituted for the subject, and the subject for the attribute; and it is *accidental* when a part only of the attribute takes the place of the subject.

The following rules must be observed in the conversion of propositions:

Rule I. The quality and the quantity of the proposition must be retained in the conversion.

Rule II. A universal negative proposition and a particular affirmative proposition may both be converted by simple conversion: for, in the first, both terms are universal (2d Axiom), and in the second, both are particular (1st Axiom); consequently, the quality and the quantity are kept in the conversion. Examples of simple conversion:

No man is a stone; no stone is a man,

Some men are good persons; some good persons are men.

Rule III. A universal affirmative proposition cannot be converted by simple conversion, for its attribute is a particular term (1st Axiom); except in necessary and reciprocal statements, that is, when they are identical in regard to the sense, as is the case in definitions. For example, "All priests are men" is not equivalent to "All men are priests" but to "Some men are priests." But "All circles are round" is equivalent to its reciprocal, "All round figures are circles."

Rule IV. A particular negative proposition cannot

be converted either simply or accidentally; for such a conversion would violate the first rule, by changing the quality or the quantity of one of the terms.

§ II. Opposition of Propositions.

When I say "Peter is a learned man," and "Peter is not a learned man," I have two propositions which are *opposite*.

Opposition is, therefore, the negation in one proposition, and the affirmation in another, of the same attribute, concerning the same subject and with the same reference. Consequently, in these two propositions, "Peter is good" and "Paul is not good," there is no opposition; nor is there any opposition in the following, "Peter is learned in philosophy" and "Peter is not learned in theology." To conclude, two propositions are in opposition when one of them denies what the other affirms. It follows that two negative propositions cannot be in opposition.

Two propositions are said to be *contrary* when in one of them more is said than is necessary to refute the other. Example: "All men are just. No man is just."

Two propositions are called *contradictory* when in one is said precisely what is necessary to refute the other; as, "All men are just. A certain man is not just."

Evidently, two contradictory propositions cannot both be either true or false; for, if so, the same thing would be and not be at the same time; that is, the same attribute would be consistent and not consistent with the subject, which is absurd.

As a corollary, since two contradictory propositions cannot be true and false at the same time, it follows that when one is true the other is false, and vice versa.

Two contrary propositions cannot both be true at the same time, but both may be false: for, as two contradictory propositions cannot both be true at the same time, since in one of them is said precisely what is sufficient for the refutation of the other; so, *a fortiori*, two contrary propositions cannot both be true at the same time, since in one of those propositions more is said than is needed for the refutation of the other: also, since, in one of the two contrary propositions more is said than is necessary to refute the other, there may be a middle term which is the true one; and consequently the two contrary propositions may both be false.

Examples: "All men are just. No man is just,"—both false. The middle term, "some men," is the true subject; and "some men are just" is the true proposition.

THIRD DISSERTATION.
ON REASONING.

When after comparing several judgments we draw a conclusion from them we are said to reason. *Reasoning* is, therefore, an act of the mind deducing a judgment from other judgments; and when expressed in words it forms an *Argument*. Argument then is to reasoning what the proposition is to judgment, namely, its formal expression in words.

Reasoning is said to be *immediate* when no comparison is needed, and *mediate* when a comparison is necessary.

Reasoning affects only *formal* truth; hence, if we assume a false principle we shall, by good reasoning, deduce a false conclusion.

There are many sorts of argument, of which the syllogism is the most common.

We shall divide this dissertation into five chapters. In the first we shall treat of the syllogism and its rules; in the second, of the different kinds of syllogisms; in the third, of the forms of argument other than the syllogism; in the fourth, of sophisms; and in the fifth, of the sources of sophisms.

CHAPTER FIRST.

OF THE SYLLOGISM AND ITS RULES.

The syllogism is an argument consisting of three propositions so arranged that from the first two, called the premises, the third necessarily follows as a conclusion.

In every syllogism there are three terms, the *major*, or greater, the *minor*, or less, and the *middle*.

The major term is the attribute of the conclusion, of which the minor is the subject: as we have already learned, the attribute is always a greater term than the subject. The middle term, which is the term of comparison, is not found in the conclusion.

The first proposition of the syllogism is called the *major* proposition, because it contains the major term; the second is called the *minor*, because it contains the minor term; and the third, which, as we have just seen, contains both the major and the minor term, is called the *conclusion.*

The major and the minor are together called the *premises,* or the *antecedent;* and the conclusion is also called the *consequent.*

Example:

Major. Middle Term. ALL BAD MEN Major Term. ARE MISERABLE; ⎫ Premises, or
Minor. Minor Term. ALL TYRANTS Middle Term. ARE BAD MEN; ⎭ Antecedents.

Conclusion. All tyrants are miserable. Consequent.

The minor premise may precede the major.

Rules of the Syllogism:

1st. The syllogism must have but three terms.

2d. No term must be greater in the conclusion than it is in the premises.

3d. The middle term must be at least once a general term.

4th. No conclusion can be deduced from two premises which are either negative or particular.

5th. Two affirmative propositions cannot produce a negative conclusion.

6th. The conclusion follows the weaker premise. That is, when one of the premises is a negative proposition the conclusion will be negative, and when one of the premises is a particular proposition the conclusion will be particular.

Examples of faulty syllogisms:

Against Rule 1st.

Every *man* is a *spirit;*

Every *substance* is *divisible*.—Four terms, no conclusion.

Against Rule 2d.

Every animal is a living being;
Every animal is a substance;
Every substance is a living being.

Every substance, in the conclusion, is a general term, and it is a particular one in the minor.

Against Rule 3d.

Every man is *an animal;*
Every brute is *an animal;*
Every man is a brute.

The middle term is taken twice in a particular sense and with a different reference, which constitutes two different terms, consequently, there are four terms in the premises.

Against Rule 4th.

No man is a stone;
Man is not marble.—No conclusion.

Against Rule 6th.

The Italians are soft;
The Italians are men;
Hence (some) men are soft.

This syllogism is good, but the following would be wrong:

No man is a stone.
Marble is stone.
Marble is man.

Syllogisms may be divided into four classes according to the position of the middle term.

In the first class—The middle term is the subject of the major and the attribute of the minor.

In the second class—The middle term is the attribute of both premises.

In the third class—The middle term is the subject of both premises.

In the fourth class—The middle term is the attribute of the major and the subject of the minor.

In the first two classes we may have four cases, or forms of syllogism; in the third class we may have six forms; and in the fourth, five forms. Each of these cases, or forms, is designated by a word containing three vowels. The first two vowels indicate the quantity of the premises, and the third indicates the quantity of the consequent.

There are, as we have seen, four kinds of propositions, which are indicated as follows:

1st. Universal affirmative—by the vowel *a*.
2d. Particular affirmative—by the vowel *i*.
3d. Universal negative—by the vowel *e*.
4th. Particular negative—by the vowel *o*.

We will illustrate the use of these vowels by two examples:

First. All VIRTUOUS MEN (Middle) are happy;
All good men are VIRTUOUS (Middle);
All good men are happy.
} One form of the first class.

Second.
No vicious conduct is PRAISEWORTHY (Middle);
All truly heroic conduct is PRAISEWORTHY (Middle);
No truly heroic conduct is vicious.
} One form of the second class.

In the first example, both of the premises and the conclusion are universal affirmative propositions, and, by the notation given above, must each be indicated by the vowel *a*. Hence the word used to designate this example must contain the vowel *a* three times. *Barbara* is the word used for this purpose.

In the second example, the major premise is universal negative, and therefore indicated by *e;* the minor is universal affirmative, and hence indicated by *a;* while the conclusion, universal negative, is designed by *e:* the word *celarent*, therefore, designates the form represented by this example.

It will now be enough, without further explanation, to give the words used to designate each form in the four classes of syllogisms:

1st Class.	2d Class.	3d Class.	4th Class.
Barbara,	Celarent,	Darapti,	Bramantip,
Cesare,	Camestres,	Disamis,	Camenes,
Darii,	Festino,	Datisi,	Dimaris,
Ferio.	Fakoro.	Felapton,	Fesapo,
		Dokamo,	Fresison.
		Feriso.	

CHAPTER SECOND.

Of the Different Sorts of Syllogisms.

The syllogism may be simple, complex, or compound. The *simple* syllogism is that of which we have treated in the preceding chapter. A *complex* syllogism is one whose conclusion contains complex terms; it may always be reduced to a simple syllogism.

Example:

Complex.
{ Divine law obliges us to honor the pastors of the Church;
Benedict is a pastor of the Church;
Hence, divine law obliges us to honor him.

This syllogism is equivalent to the following:

Simple.
{ Our pastors ought to be honored;
Benedict is our pastor;
Hence, he ought to be honored.

The syllogism is *compound* when the major is a conditional, disjunctive, or negative conjunctive proposition.

I. The major is *conditional* when it consists of two parts, the one called the antecedent and the other the consequent, united by *if*. In this case, when we concede the antecedent in the minor we must affirm the consequent in the conclusion, and when we deny the consequent in the minor we must also deny the antecedent in the conclusion—*verum prius, ergo et posterius; falsum consequens, ergo et antecedens*—that is, the first being true, the second is true; and the second being false, the first is also false.

Example:
If Peter is wise he will stay away from gambling houses;

1st. But Peter is wise; hence, he will stay away, &c.

2d. But Peter will not stay away, &c.; hence, Peter is not, &c.

II. The major is *disjunctive* when it consists of two or more parts incompatible with one another, and united by *either—or*. In this case, when one part is affirmed in the minor the other is denied in the conclusion. The parts forming the major must be contradictory propositions.

Example:

We must either restrain our passions or yield to them;

But we must restrain them (since reason and religion teach us to do so);

Hence, we must not yield to them.

Since the two propositions forming the major ought to be contradictories, there should be no middle term between them.

Example:

We must either obey governments commanding evil to be done, or we must revolt against them;

But we must not obey governments commanding evil, &c.;

Hence, we must revolt against them.

Here, the major term, which should consist of two contradictories, is made up of two contraries, both of which, as we have seen, may be false; hence the error in this example. The truth is contained in a middle proposition, "We must suffer persecution."

III. The major is *negative conjunctive* when it consists of two contrary propositions. In this case, when we affirm in the minor we must deny in the conclusion, for both propositions cannot be true; but if we deny in the minor we cannot absolutely affirm in the conclusion, for two contrary propositions may both be false. The rule is, therefore, as follows: One part ought to be affirmed in the minor and the other denied in the conclusion.

Example:
No one can serve God and mammon;
The avaricious man serves mammon;
Hence, he does not serve God.

CHAPTER THIRD.

OF THE FORMS OF ARGUMENT OTHER THAN THE SYLLOGISM.

1st. The *Enthymeme.*—This is an abbreviated syllogism, in which one of the premises is omitted.

Example:
God is good;
Hence he should be loved.

The major, "We should love those who are good," is omitted.

2d. The *Epichireme.*—This is a syllogism whose major and minor are accompanied with proofs. The substance of Cicero's beautiful "Oration for Milo" is given in the following Epichireme:

It is lawful to kill those who lie in wait to kill us (this is proved by the natural law and by the laws of nations—many examples);

But Clodius lay in wait to kill Milo (this is proved by the number of armed men who accompanied Clodius, his absence from Rome at the time of the attack, &c.);

Hence, it was lawful for Milo to kill Clodius.

An Epichireme may be reduced to a simple syllogism.

3d. The *Sorites.*—This is an accumulation of propositions, so connected that the attribute of each is made the subject of that which follows, and the subject of the first becomes the attribute of the last.

The propositions must be well "chained," so that there may be no middle term between the attribute of one proposition and the subject of the following; and no equivocal proposition should be employed.

Example:

Avaricious men desire many things,

Those who desire many things are in need of many things,

Those who are in need of many things are dissatisfied with their condition,

Those who are dissatisfied with their condition are not happy;

Hence, avaricious men are not happy.

4th. The *Dilemma*.—This is an argument in which we conclude of the whole major, which is generally a disjunctive proposition, what we have concluded of each part. It is called a horned argument, because it strikes on both sides.

Example:

When the wicked die, either they are utterly destroyed or their souls are immortal:

If they are utterly destroyed there is no hope of eternal happiness for them;

If their souls are immortal there is also no hope of eternal happiness for them, since God is just;

Hence, there is no hope of happiness for the wicked after death.

To have the dilemma good no middle term must be possible in the major, and the conclusion must be true after each part.

5th. *Induction* or *Enumeration.*—This is an argument in which the major is an enumeration of particulars, from which a universal conclusion is deduced. That the argument may be absolutely conclusive, the enumeration must be complete.

6th. The *Example.*—This is a common form of argument in which a single conclusion is drawn from a single proposition. This may be done in three ways: by similitude, or comparison (*a pari*), by opposition, or contrast (*e contrario*), and by superiority (*a fortiori*).

Examples:

1st. *a pari.* God forgave David when he repented; *a pari*, He will forgive me.

2d. *e contrario.* Intemperance is hurtful to health; *e contrario*, Temperance is favorable to health.

3d. *a fortiori.* John's conversation for even one hour is tedious; *a fortiori*, it would be tedious for a whole day.

CHAPTER FOURTH.

OF SOPHISMS.

The word *sophism* comes from the Greek *sophizo*, which signifies *to teach wisdom;* and the Greek noun *sophismos* means *wise invention.* From this etymology it is easy to understand that the word sophism had not in the beginning the meaning which it has at present. Men of subtle intellects, falsely called philosophers, have abused their powers of reasoning so far as to construct a theory for reasoning falsely, a theory by which fallacies are logically established as if they were truths. This is what is now called sophistry. A *sophism*, then, is a false reasoning, with the intention of deceiving. When the sophism results from ignorance in the reasoner, it is called a *paralogism*.

Aristotle divides sophisms into three classes: 1st. formal sophisms; 2d. material sophisms, or sophisms *extra dictionem;* and 3d. verbal sophisms, *in dictione*, that is, sophisms existing in the words used.

Formal sophisms are syllogisms badly constructed. Of these we have already spoken.

Material sophisms are the following:

(a) *Ignorantia elenchi*, which may be translated, "ignorance of the subject." This occurs when we prove what is not in question, or what is not denied by our opponents; also when we suppose them to be actuated by principles which they disavow, or when we draw from their words or actions inferences which they would not admit. This sophism is of common occurrence; it comes from precipitation, prejudice, and feelings of pride or hatred towards our opponents, but still more from equivocation in terms not well defined. In order to avoid this last source of error, we must know both the precise sense and the exact extent of the expressions used by our opponents.

(b) *Petitio principii*, or "begging the question." This species of false reasoning takes place when we suppose as proved that which is to be proved. There is no substantial difference between this sophism and that called the vicious circle (*circulus vitiosus*), or arguing in a circle, which consists in proving two propositions by one another, neither of them being otherwise proved.

Examples:

The earth is immovable, because the sun moves around it.

Evidence is infallible, because God is infinitely true; and God is infinitely true, because it is evident, &c.

(c) *Non causa pro causa*, or "Not the cause for the cause." This sophism occurs whenever we give as the cause of some effect that which is not its cause. This happens frequently, especially in the case of "*Post hoc, ergo propter hoc*,"—after this, therefore on account of this.

(d) Imperfect enumeration. No explanation needs to be given of this kind of false argument.

(e) Fallacy of objection. This sophism results when we consider as a cause, or as an essential, that which is only an accident.

The following are examples of the fallacy of objection:

(1) Philosophy rendered many men impious; then philosophy is a bad thing.

(2) False miracles have been believed; then no faith ought to be given to miracles, &c.

Verbal sophisms, or sophisms *in dictione*, are the following:

(a) Fallacy of division and composition. Passing from a distributive to a collective sense in the use of words.

Example:

Two and one are even and odd;

But two and one are three;
Therefore three is even and odd.

One and two are even and odd when divided (*in sensu diviso*), but not when united (*in sensu composito*). This distinction is the only one to be given in such cases. We may see that in the above sophism there are four terms: two and one are taken *in sensu diviso*, or distributively, in the major; and *in sensu composito*, or collectively, in the minor. Hence the syllogism involves an error against the 1st rule.

2d. Passing from a collective to a distributive sense; or attributing to several parts of a collection what is true only of the collection itself.

Example:

The Apostles were twelve;
Peter and James were Apostles;
Therefore Peter and James were twelve.

Here again we have four terms in the premises. The Apostles are taken together (*in sensu composito*) in the major; and separately (*in sensu diviso*) in the minor,—and no conclusion can be drawn.

(b) **Fallacy of accident.** This consists in asserting something of a subject in a general sense, in one of the premises; while in the other premise we connect with that subject some accidental peculiarity.

Example:

You now have the same feet that you always had;
But you once had small feet;
Therefore you now have small feet.

Putting this sophism in the form of a regular syllogism, we shall perceive that there are four terms in the premises.

Your present feet are those of your childhood;
The feet of your childhood were small feet;
Therefore your present feet are small feet.

In the major, the "feet of childhood" means the *essence* of those feet, while in the minor it means their *form* or *shape*. Hence the middle term being taken in two different senses we have four terms in the premises and can draw no conclusion.

Besides these two kinds of verbal sophisms, we have (c) that of Equivocation, (d) that of Amphibology, and (e) that of Figure.

Example of a sophism of figure:
No creature laughs but man;
But a meadow laughs;
Hence a meadow is a man.

We may observe that "meadow" is first taken in a figurative sense and then in a literal.

Doctor Ubaghs, speaking of these last three sophisms (c, d, and e), says that they do not deserve to be mentioned, since they could embarrass no one but a child or a person of very dull mind.

CHAPTER FIFTH.

Of the Sources of Sophisms.

The sources of sophisms are:

1st. Precipitation. We are liable to commit a sophism whenever we pronounce a judgment on anything which we have not well considered or which is not sufficiently well known.

2d. Prejudice. In this case we form a judgment in accordance with our wishes and without previous examination.

3d. Our passions. There are impressions violently agitating our mind and forcing it in different directions.

4th. Our senses. The senses have been given to us by God that we may judge of external bodies, not as they are in themselves, but as they appear to us.

5th. Our imagination. The imagination is that faculty of the mind which pictures to itself material objects that do not affect the senses.

Although the human mind is very imperfect, still it would never be deceived if we always acted prudently in the investigation of truth, abstaining from judging until the truth shows itself manifestly to the mind. We should then be ignorant of many things, and know others imperfectly; but we should not err.

FOURTH DISSERTATION.

ON METHOD.

We have now explained the notions of Ideas, the nature of Judgment and of Reasoning, and we have given rules for judging and reasoning correctly. It remains for us to examine in what order we should arrange these mental operations for the investigation and manifestation of truth. This arrangement and order is called Method, or "The way we must go in order to reach the end we have in view."

Definition.—*Method* is that operation of the mind by which we dispose our thoughts in that order which is most suitable for detecting the truth which we do not know and showing it as soon as we know it.

Evidently the necessity of method shows the weakness of our mind; but without it progress cannot be made, nor can pleasure be found, in the reading of books or the teaching of masters.

Method being the application of the science of logic, is consequently an art; and this art is acquired rather by practice and experience than by precept, and it depends more on the rectitude and attention of our mind than on rules.

Division.—Some authors divide method into two kinds, the analytic and the synthetic. This division cannot be accepted; for, according to it, the analytic method, which is the same as the method of induction, would proceed always by analysis; but this would too much restrict the method of induction, in which we have to proceed as much by synthesis as by analysis, as experience shows. We must then take a more accurate division.

There are two divisions of method, or two methods; the method of invention, which comprises observation and induction; and the method of demonstration, or dialectics.

1st Division, the Method of Invention.

The difference between observation and induction may be stated thus: When our attention is directed towards a phenomenon or a fact, in order only to know it, we make an observation; but when that attention is directed to the same fact or phenomenon, in order to discover some law, or to deduce some conclusion from principles, we make, in the first case, an induction, and in the second, a deduction.

Observation is consequently a serious attention of the mind, in order to know some fact, which fact may be either exterior or interior.

In order to observe well, four operations are necessary: First, attention; and this attention must be intense, persevering, and free from prejudice; second, distinct perception of the fact, that is, we must determine well the circumstances of its existence, and its essential elements; third, analysis, which should be complete, the examination being minute and exhaustive; and fourth, synthesis, which should also be complete, the recapitulation being made in proper order. These rules ought to be followed not only in observing but also in making experiments.

Induction, which always supposes previous observation, is an operation of the mind inducing us to affirm of things not observed that which we have observed in similar things.

Four conditions are necessary in order that the induction may be good: "First, *abstraction;* second, *comparison;* third, *generalization* (This, as we have seen, signifies the discovery of a quality common to several similar objects; and this common quality serves as a distinguishing mark for the class in which all the similar objects are contained. *Classification* is the formation of these classes, and we may see that generalization affords the materials for classification.); and fourth, *induction*, properly so called, which is the extension of the common quality discovered by generalization to other objects of a similar kind.

Note.—This method leads us to a certain knowledge of the truth. There are other modes of investigation which lead us, not to a sure, but to a more or less probable knowledge of the truth; these are: analogy, hypothesis and the calculation of probabilities.

Analogy is an operation of the mind attributing to one object some quality observed in another.

Example: A certain medicine has proved to be good for a certain sick person; analogy would lead us to believe that it would be good for another person sick in like manner.

Analogy must be grounded on obvious resemblance, and the resemblance must have necessary connection with the conclusion which we draw. Hence the science called cranioscopy, and others of that kind, are false.

Hypothesis is the supposition of a cause, in order to explain several effects of which the cause is concealed. An hypothesis is also called a *postulate*.

Example: The hypothesis of the existence of a neutral electric fluid in all bodies, in order to explain electric phenomena.

Hypotheses are very useful, but subject to many serious inconveniences. In order to proceed wisely when we form an hypothesis, we must first examine well the case which we wish to explain by hypothesis, and notice all its circumstances; for the degree of probability of an hypothesis depends on the number of circumstances which it explains: and, in the second place, we should chose out of those circumstances that which is most important, and try to explain it by the hypothesis; but although our hypothesis may explain this most important circumstance, yet if it be in contradiction to any other circumstance it must be rejected.

The *calculation of probabilities*, so far as it has reference to philosophy, will be spoken of in several other places, especially in Ethics.

2D DIVISION, THE METHOD OF DEMONSTRATION, OR DIALECTICS.

To demonstrate is to prove; and a *demonstration* is an argument in which the truth of a proposition is deduced from one or more propositions which are known to be true. The proposition from which the conclusion is drawn is called the principle of the demonstration; and as this principle may be either sure or probable, the deduction will be accordingly either certain or only probable.

The parts of a demonstration are as follows:

1st. The question, or proposition to be demonstrated. When the question is concerning a truth to be demonstrated, it is called a *theorem*, a *thesis*, or simply a *proposition;* and when it is concerning a truth to be discovered, it is called a *problem*. The question must be defined, divided into its parts, precise, and well arranged.

Example: The question is, is the human soul immortal? Immortality must be defined; and the question must be divided into its two parts concerning internal immortality and external immortality.

The first part of the question may be passed over, as evident; and then the real question comes, which is, whether the soul, after the death of the body, will pass to another life, a life without end. We next arrange this question into its two parts, (a) whether the soul, on leaving the body, will pass to another life, and (b) whether that life is eternal.

2d. The principle of the demonstration. This principle, or these principles, must be certain and connected with the question. They may be axioms, or facts of experience, or simply postulates. These two first parts, the question and the principle, are called the *matter* of the demonstration.

3d. The form of the demonstration, or the connection of the conclusion with the principle. This connection must first be accurate, that is, nothing should be used in the argument which does not belong to the question; and second, it must be clear.

The demonstration may be:

1st. *Analytical*, ascending, going from the question to some general principle; or *synthetical*, descending, starting from some general principle and coming to the question.

2d. *Direct*, or *indirect*.

3d. *A priori*, the effects being proved by the cause; or *a posteriori*, the cause being proved by the effects.

4th. *Absolute*, resulting from a true principle; or *relative*, grounded on a principle admitted as true by our opponent, whether really true or not. This last demonstration does not prove that the conclusion is absolutely true, but only that it cannot be denied by those who admit the principle on which it is based: it is therefore called the *argumentum ad hominem*.

FIFTH DISSERTATION.

ON CERTITUDE.

CHAPTER FIRST.

PRELIMINARY NOTIONS—DEFINITIONS.

Certitude is the firm adhesion of the mind to the truth made known to it. Certitude is at the same time a state and an act of the mind. As a state it may be defined to be, a disposition by which the mind tends to adhere firmly to the known truth.

Truth is, "that which is." Truth is either necessary or contingent. *Necessary truth* is that which cannot but be, and which cannot but be as it is. Such is the truth of the existence of God.

A *contingent truth* is one which, although it may exist, yet might not have existed, or might have existed in a different manner.

Truth cannot be known by the intellect unless it is cognoscible. That by which truth is cognoscible, or rendered capable of being perceived by the intellect, is called *evidence*. Evidence has an objective sense, as the term has been used by all good philosophers; although some have pretended that evidence being a perception has only a subjective sense.

Certitude is *subjective* when considered as existing in the mind; and it is *objective* when considered as existing in the object, in which case it is the same as truth itself, inasmuch as it is surely known, or inasmuch as it is the object of our certitude.

Evidently subjective certitude cannot exist without the objective, but objective certitude may exist without the subjective.

Evidence is also subjective as well as objective. Objective evidence is that which is perceived by the mind; it is objective evidence that is defined above. Objective evidence is the *visibility of truth*, and subjective evidence is the *vision of truth*.

Certitude is *implicit*, that is direct, common or spontaneous, when the mind adheres to the truth from what is only an implicit knowledge of the motion or cause which determines that adhesion. Certitude is *explicit*, philosophical or scientific, when the mind adheres to the truth from an explicit knowledge of the motion or cause which determines that adhesion. Both implicit and explicit certitude are true.

Certitude is *immediate* when the evidence of the truth is intuitive, and *mediate* when the evidence is discursive, or the result of a course of reasoning.

Evidence is itself immediate or intuitive when a truth manifests itself to the mind without the aid of another truth, as in the axiom. The whole is greater than any of its parts; and it is mediate or discursive when truth is made manifest by the aid of reasoning.

NOTE.—Mediate evidence is formed from that which is immediate, and requires more labor from our minds for its perception.

It is not possible by noting the manner in which the perception takes place in our mind to fix the line between intuitive and discursive evidence; we must, for this purpose, accept the definitions and take them as rules for making the distinction between the two kinds of evidence.

A *primary truth* is one which is intuitively evident; and a *secondary truth* is one which is discursively evident.

Metaphysical certitude is that which is based upon the essence of things, and which can on no hypothesis be different from what it is.

Physical certitude is that which is based upon the laws of nature, and which cannot be other than it is except by a miracle.

Moral certitude is that which is based upon the laws of our moral constitution, and which cannot be otherwise without affecting the condition of humanity.

In regard to the subject, certitude is one and the same for all, though it admits of several degrees in the clearness of our perception of the truth and in the intensity of our adhesion to it.

CHAPTER SECOND.

OF THE CRITERION OF CERTITUDE.

A criterion is a sign by which something may be distinguished from everything else; consequently, the *criterion of certitude* is the sign by which certitude is perfectly distinguished from error. Evidently such a sign must exist, but in order to proceed methodically let us first examine what is the criterion of truth.

I. Proposition. *Objective evidence is the criterion of truth.* To prove this proposition we proceed as follows:

That which is so evidently the characteristic of truth that it cannot be attributed to falsehood, is the criterion of truth.

Such a characteristic is objective evidence,—that is, the property by which truth is cognoscible to our minds, and consequently by which truth is distinguished from what is not truth; for if evidence could be attributed to falsehood as well as to truth it would not be that by which what is true is distinguished from what is not true.

Hence, evidence, taken objectively, is the criterion of truth.

In order to meet objections that may be brought against this proposition, let us observe that there is a difference between judging and perceiving. We judge sometimes that such a thing is so and so, and perceive afterwards that we have made a mistake. In the first case we *judge* erroneously of something, which afterwards, on account of evidence, we *perceive* exactly as it is.

II. The criterion of certitude differs from the criterion of truth. The criterion of truth is the character proper to truth, and consequently something essentially objective; but the criterion of certitude is the character proper to our knowledge, and consequently something both objective and subjective. It is, after all, the criterion of truth applied to our mind, the criterion of truth being the cause of our certitude.

In order to determine in what the criterion of certitude consists, let us first see what are the conditions or marks which ought to be found in such a criterion.

This criterion ought to be: 1st, necessarily connected with truth; 2d, known by itself; and 3d, universal, that is, it ought to be the last reason of certitude.

Proposition. *A clear perception is the only criterion of certitude.* Argument:

That is a criterion of certitude which has the requisite qualities for establishing such a criterion;

But a clear perception has such qualities;

Hence, a clear perception is the criterion of certitude.

Proof of the minor. 1st. Such a clear perception has a necessary connection with truth; what we clearly perceive is evident, and it cannot be evident, as we have said, unless it be true. 2d. It is something known by itself, since it is a perception; for nothing is more known to us than what we see. 3d. It is the last reason of certitude; for the last reason which we can give for our certitude is this: "I see," "I perceive clearly."

We have said that this clear perception is the only motive of certitude; for the other motives of certitude, of which we shall speak hereafter, are all grounded on this criterion. The last reason which we bring forward is always, "I see clearly."

CHAPTER THIRD.

OF THE EXISTENCE OF CERTITUDE.

Some philosophers have altogether denied the existence of certitude, while others have established erroneous systems concerning its attributes. The following are the schools which we shall refute by the exposition of the true philosophical doctrine concerning the existence and the motives of certitude:

1st. Universal or subjective scepticism, also called Pyrrhonism. This denies, or at least doubts, the existence of subjective certitude; and since one who doubts his own existence may doubt anything this subjective scepticism is called universal scepticism.

This was the system of the sophist Pyrrho and his disciples, and also of the "new sceptics," a sect that renewed the errors of Pyrrho at the beginning of the Christian era. Among modern philosophers Montaigne, Bayle and Hume have indirectly adhered to the same system.

2nd. Objective scepticism, or Kantism. This is the doctrine of those who accept subjective, but reject objective certitude. It is the system of the modern German school, represented by Kant, Hermes and Fichte. Some French philosophers, of the school of Jouffroy, have accepted the doctrine of Kant with modifications.

3d. Idealism and Empiricism. The idealists are those philosophers who, extolling too much the certitude of pure reason, destroy in part the certitude of experience. Berkeley and Mallebranche are the chief representatives of this system. Descartes adhered more or less to the system of Mallebranche, and he was also of opinion that the perception of the senses, of itself, could not produce certitude.

The empiricists reject the certitude of pure reason, and teach that sensation is the only cause of certitude; they are also called materialists and sensists. Of this class were Condillac and Helvetius, and in our time Augustus Comte, Littre, &c.

4th. Historical scepticism. This is the system of all those who attack historical certitude. It is of two kinds, general, when it rejects all historical certitude, and particular when it refuses to admit some particular historical fact. We find this system, in regard to its principles, in Bayle, and in the writings of Craig, a Scotch mathematician, and also of Laplace and Lacroix.

A branch of this system has been called the theory of Mythism, which is mythism applied to history and religion. Philosophers, or rather infidel writers, try to explain in a mythical way the best authenticated facts of history. This system appears in the dangerous writings of Vico, Michelet, Dupuis, Volney, Strauss, Hegel, and, lately, Renan.

5th. Rationalism. This is the doctrine of those who do not admit any revealed truth, and try to explain in a natural manner the miracles and mysteries of revealed religion. We shall see hereafter that revelation is possible, that it is an infallible motive of judging, that the doctrine revealed by God may be perceived by human reason, &c.

The system of rationalism is widespread. It has been taught in France by Cousin, Jouffroy and Damiron.

6th. *Fideism.* This is the doctrine of several philosophers who think that genuine certitude cannot be obtained except by faith, either human or divine. As we may see, it is directly opposed to rationalism.

To this system belongs (a) the doctrine of Huet, who taught that reason, of itself, cannot give true certitude, but must be assisted by divine faith, and also (b) the doctrine of Lamennais, the author of the famous book "Essai sur l'Indifference," who was of opinion that what he calls "individual reason" cannot give us true certitude, but that what he calls "general reason" is necessary for this purpose. Lamennais's system is founded on a vicious circle; for the reasons which determined him to reject individual reason must also determine him to reject general reason, which, after all, is composed of individual reasons. The whole system rests upon obscure and inaccurate definitions and explanations. It created much excitement in the beginning on account of its novelty and obscurity, and also on account of the talent of its author.

6th. *Traditionalism,* or the system of those who think that tradition, that is, revelation made to man and handed down by the testimony of men, is necessary to us in order that we should have certain knowledge of truths of the natural order. Dr. Bonnetty was the author of this system, which was condemned in the provincial council of Rheims, France, in 1853, the condemnation being approved by Pope Pius IX., who, at the same time, condemned the following errors:

3*

(a) They err who teach that human reason is, by its nature, inimical to divine revelation, or opposed to it.

(b) They err who teach that the force of human reason, in the present condition of our fallen nature, has been almost destroyed, or rendered powerless.

(c) They err who teach that no interior power has been left man by which he may acquire truth, or that all truths and notions come to us from exterior source, by speech and revelation.

(d) They err who affirm that man cannot with his reasoning powers perceive and demonstrate certain truths of the metaphysical and moral order.

(e) They err who teach that man cannot naturally admit any metaphysical or moral truth, unless he has first believed by an act of supernatural faith, through divine revelation.

(f) They err who do not admit a distinction between the natural divine law and the positive divine law.

Having named and described the systems according to which certitude is either disfigured or its existence totally denied, it now remains that we should affirm and demonstrate it. For this purpose the following propositions are stated and demonstrated:

First Proposition.—Certitude Exists.

It is certain that certitude exists if there are any truths which the mind accepts without any fear of erring; for then it perceives these truths clearly, and this clear perception is the criterion of certitude.

But there are such truths; for when we say "Two and two are equal to four," the mind accepts the fact without any fear of erring. Hence certitude exists.

Second Proposition.

The existence of certitude is a fact which cannot be rigidly demonstrated, but which nevertheless becomes clearly manifest on mere statement or representation to the mind.

Certitude is a fact which cannot be demonstrated, if it be necessary for its demonstration that we should take as a principle that which is to be demonstrated. But such is the case in regard to the existence of certitude; for to demonstrate it we should first have to take as granted certain premises,—which assumption would of itself suppose the existence of certitude; but this would be the *petitio principii*, or begging the question. It is enough then to show or state the existence of certitude; for this is so clear of itself that no one can seriously doubt it when thus presented to the mind.

Third Proposition.

No one can doubt the existence of certitude without falling into a contradiction.

He who supposes in the premises what he wishes to deny in the conclusion, contradicts himself. But such is the case with one denying the existence of certitude; for his conclusion would be the affirmation of his belief in the non-existence of certitude, and as an affirmation is the expression of a certitude it follows that he contradicts himself.

Sceptics bring many objections against this thesis. They say that we may find arguments both for and against every proposition, and that therefore we must doubt; and, again, that the human mind is fallible and knows nothing fully, and that for this reason also we should doubt. It is true that we must sometimes doubt, but not always; and hence certitude does exist. When they add that perhaps life is a dream, we need not stop to answer them.

This thesis refutes both subjective and objective scepticism.

CHAPTER FOURTH.

Of the Motives of Certitude.

A *motive*, in general, is that which disposes the mind to adhere firmly to some truth. We have seen that evidence clearly perceived is the general motive of certitude; but this evidence affects the mind diversely in regard to its adhesion to the truth, according to the different orders of truth. Hence, there are different motives, which we shall examine successively:

First Motive.—The Certitude of Pure Reason.

Pure reason, or simply reason, is the faculty by which our mind perceives what is absolutely necessary. We have already seen what is meant by a necessary truth, and have shown that the evidence which pertains to necessary truth is the evidence of contradiction, that is, an evidence which does not allow us to suppose that the truth is other than it is without contradicting ourselves, or saying implicitly that the same thing may be and not be at the same time.

Reason has for its principle all necessary truths, that is all truths which are intuitively evident. These truths are the sources from which all other truths are derived, and it is on this account that they are called the principles of pure reason. These principles have been also called axioms; and, although some writers have made a distinction between axioms and principles, we shall consider the two words as synonimous.

We may define an *axiom*, or *principle of pure reason*, to be a necessary and self-evident truth, from which other truths proceed.

These principles are: 1st. The principle of identity or essence; namely, "What is, is." This is the same as the principle of contradiction; namely, "The same thing cannot be and not be at the same time," a principle implicitly contained in every necessary truth. 2nd. The principle of equality and inequality; namely, "Two things which are each equal to a third are equal to each other," and "Two things, of which one is equal to a third, while the other is not equal to this third, are unequal to each other." 3d. The principle of substance; namely, "The mode supposes the substance." 4th. The principle of casuality; namely, "That which has a beginning has a cause."

These axioms being given, we prove the following

Proposition.—*Pure reason gives certitude of necessary truths.*

(a) This proposition is clear according to the

very definition of reason. Reason is a perception; but if the mind could never adhere to truth, reason would at the same time be a perception and not a perception. It would be a perception according to the hypothesis, and it would not be a perception because we should always doubt; that is, the same thing would, at the same time, both be and not be, which involves a contradiction. Hence, when reason perceives clearly it gives true certitude.

(b) This proposition cannot be seriously opposed, if it be false argument to suppose as true what we attack as false. But such is the case with any argument contrived against the legitimacy of reason, since he who would argue against reason would suppose that reasoning is a lawful mode for the attainment of certitude.

Second Motive.—Consciousness.

Consciousness is the interior feeling by which our mind is aware of its present condition or state.

Proposition.—*Consciousness produces a true certitude in regard to our interior feelings and affections.*

Consciousness gives a true certitude, if there is a necessary connection between it and the truth of the judgments formed by it. But such is the case, since the object and the subject are the same individual; consequently, consciousness cannot be deceived, although it may deceive. Hence consciousness gives true certitude; and the judgments formed by it concerning the appearances of things which have affected it are essentially true, since they express the present state of the soul.

Here again, we cannot demonstrate the truth, but simply show it; for any truth which we could bring forward as a principle of demonstration would rest on reason and on consciousness, which latter is aware of the evidence produced in our mind. These two motives, reason and consciousness, are, as we see, chained together.

Our own existence is, in regard to ourselves, the first truth known of itself, or self-evident.

THIRD MOTIVE.—THE EVIDENCE OF THE SENSES.

The evidence of the senses is that invincible propensity which induces us to refer our sensations to the bodies which, according to our convictions, have been the causes of them; and by which, therefore, we judge of the existence of the bodies themselves.

Our senses lead us into many errors and illusions, and consequently some philosophers have refused to acknowledge that our senses may give us true certitude. Hence the origin of objective scepticism, of idealism and of traditionalism. Against those philosophers we establish the following

Proposition.—*By the evidence of the senses we can judge infallibly of the existence of bodies in general.*

That is infallibly true which we are irresistibly forced by nature to believe as true. But we are irresistibly forced by nature to believe in the truth of the existence of bodies in general, which we perceive by our senses. Hence, by the evidence of the senses we can judge infallibly of the existence of bodies in general.

We prove the minor as follows: A propensity

which is universal, constant, and irresistible may be considered to be the effect of truth, or the voice of nature, and consequently to exclude every doubt. But that propensity by which we are led to judge of the existence of bodies in general is universal, constant and irresistible. It is universal, since we find it in all men; constant, for all men have it during their whole life; and irresistible, since we cannot overcome it whatever efforts we make. It is then the voice of nature, the expression of truth.

Indirect demonstration.—If there were no bodies, there would be no difference between the phantoms of our imagination and real bodies; but we know that this difference does exist, and hence bodies must exist.

The evidence of the senses, according to the more probable opinion, gives immediate certitude; and, consequently, in regard to the strength of the conviction produced in our mind, the certitude given by the evidence of the senses is equal to that given by reason or by consciousness, from which it differs only in regard to the object, which is metaphysical in one case and physical in the other.

The propensity by which we are led to believe in the existence of bodies in general, will also enable us to judge in favor of the existence of bodies and external events, in particular; for the same argument may be brought forward in this second part of the thesis as in the first. But in this case four conditions are required in order that the evidence of the senses may be an infallible motive of certitude:

1st. The organs of sense must be sound and in their normal condition.

2nd. The bodies themselves must be within the limits of the perception of our senses.

3d. Nothing must intervene between the organs of sense and the bodies, so as to interfere with the ordinary laws of their action.

4th. Each of the senses must be exerted upon an object upon which it can properly act.

These conditions being observed, the evidence of the senses gives a true certitude in judging of the relative properties of bodies in particular, but not of their essence; that is, we may judge of them as they appear to us, but not as they are in themselves.

Fourth Motive.—The Consent of Mankind in Things of the Moral Order.

By the *consent of mankind*, we do not mean unanimity, or metaphysical universality, but that general consent which is called moral, being the consent of the greater and sounder part of mankind.

This consent is the result of common sense, and *common sense* is nothing else than that general knowledge of first notions or principles which is found in all men.

In order that such a consent may be a criterion of certitude, it must be constant, uniform, reasonable, and not indifferent in regard to its object.

Proposition.—*The consent of mankind, with the conditions prescribed above, is an infallible motive of judging, in regard to several moral truths.*

1st. Either such a consent ought to be admitted as a criterion of certitude, or some private opinion should be preferred to it; but such a preference would be absurd, and therefore the general consent must be admitted.

2nd. A man who would defend an opinion contrary to common sense ought to defend it with irresistible arguments; but he could not find such arguments, (a) in his reason, for his reason must be in harmony with universal reason; nor (b) in the consent of mankind, for he rejects this motive of certitude: he would, then, be obliged to admit this consent or be in contradiction with himself.

3d. Direct argument.—It would be absurd to admit that the majority of men, and most sound part of humanity, would deceive, or could be deceived; but if one should deny the proposition under consideration this absurdity would result. Consequently the general consent must be accepted as an expression of the truth.

4th. This consent has been accepted in all ages and at all times as an infallible motive of judging. To show this, it will be sufficient to quote the following from Cicero: "What is established upon the laws of nature must be true, if anything is true; but a general consent of mankind, which is constant, uniform, and refers to something of great importance, as the existence of a Supreme Being, the necessity of worshiping the Deity, &c., is the voice of nature.

To solve any objections to this proposition, we have only to refer to the four conditions already indicated.

Fifth Motive.—The Testimony of Men.

As we have already said, we can judge by our senses only of those facts which we have witnessed: for other facts we must rely on the testimony of men. But, by its nature, such testimony is not necessarily infallible; and we have to examine under what conditions it may be considered an infallible motive of certitude. We shall first give some general notions concerning the *facts*, the *witnesses*, and the *conditions* which the testimony must have in order to be an infallible motive of certitude.

(A) The facts may be first, contemporaneous or past; second, public or private; third, of great or of little importance; fourth, favorable to the views of the people, or opposed to them; fifth, clear or obscure; and sixth, natural or supernatural.

(B) The witnesses may be, first, eye-witnesses or historical witnesses; and second, contemporaneous with the events or posterior to them.

(C) The testimony, in order to be an infallible motive of certitude, must have the following conditions: First, the fact must be possible; second, it must be important; third, there must be several witnesses who were not deceived, who would not deceive, and who could not deceive, even if they wished; and fourth, these witnesses must speak clearly and be clearly understood.

Bayle and his followers have attacked the legitimacy of the testimony of men as an infallible motive of certitude, and have gone so far as to deny the possibility of establishing with certainty the truth of any historical fact. This system has been called Historical Pyrrhonism; and it must be rejected, for the following reasons: First, it is as much repugnant to the nature and moral disposition of men as is Universal Scepticism; second, it is opposed to reason, which naturally admits that several witnesses cannot be deceived in regard to the substance of an important fact, and that they would not and could not deceive: this second part is grounded (a) on the love of truth which is natural to man and (b) on the principle of veracity or the inclination which all men have to speak this truth: the impossibility of deceiving may come from the fact itself, and this takes place when many relate a fact which is hurtful or useless to them, or one concerning which their previous interests are divided; or the impossibility may come from the nature of the testimony, as when many persons relate the event in the same way, even in the smallest details; or, again, it may come from the character of the witnesses, and is very clear when they are all honest.

Pyrrhonism must, in the third place, be rejected because its acceptance would result in the subversion of religion, of society and of private rights. The truth of religion is established by facts; while society rests upon a system of customs, laws and forms of government, which, in regard to their origin, are based on tradition, or the testimony of men; and private rights, so far as their origin is concerned, depend upon titles and documents handed down from generation to generation by the testimony of men. Bayle's doctrine must therefore be rejected.

From what has been said, it is indirectly proved that the testimony of men is sufficient authority for the existence of facts of which we have not been eye-witnesses, including historical facts.

We have now to proceed to the direct proof of the proposition that the testimony of men is an infallible motive of certitude in regard to facts. As the facts may be either natural or supernatural, it is evident that the question at issue is a double one; we shall therefore examine it in two sections.

§ I. Authority of the testimony of men concerning natural facts.

1st. Proposition.—*The testimony of men is an infallible motive of judging of contemporaneous facts.*

We may judge that a fact is true when the witnesses have not been deceived, and when they would not and could not deceive. But such is the case with facts which are contemporaneous and of great importance. This minor has been fully developed in the preceding remarks; therefore the testimony of men is an infallible motive, &c.

NOTE.—When we speak of facts we mean the substance of them, for we may be deceived in regard to secondary circumstances.

It is not necessary that the number of the witnesses should be great, provided, 1st, that they are honest, 2nd, that their account is uniform, 3d, that they persevere in giving the same testimony at all times, and 4th, that it is evident they are not influenced by motives of interest or pleasure, or that their interests are divided, or that the fact is opposed to their interests, or that the fact is of such notoriety that any fraud might be detected by other contemporary witnesses.

We may accept the evidence of even one eye-witness when he is entirely trustworthy and when the fact which he relates is in necessary connection with other known facts, and especially when the witness is of great wisdom and virtue, and still more if he attests by miracles the truth of his testimony.

The objections to this first proposition, given under different forms, are expressed in the following major: "If the testimony of one man gives only probability, the testimony of several men will give only several probabilities, but no certainty." We deny the major; the amount of probabilities is not to the point: the question is not concerning the value of testimonies taken separately, but concerning the value of testimonies taken together. Consequently the objection is a sophism, which we have called *ignorantia elenchi*, or a mistaking of the question at issue.

2d. Proposition.—*The testimony of men is sometimes an infallible motive of judging of past events.*

Argument: The testimony of men is an infallible motive of judging of past facts, provided there be several means by which truth comes to us. But such is the case, the means being: tradition, history and monuments.

The force of the argument from tradition comes, first, from the moral impossibility that many men have been deceived, or that they have deceived; this has been sufficiently developed already: and, second, from the argument of prescription, according to which the actual existence of a tradition or a universal custom, the reason for which cannot be given unless the fact on which it is based be accepted, makes it necessary to accept the fact; for such a tradition could not originate in error or falsehood, it not being possible in regard to facts of a serious nature and having a serious consequence, that an error should have either suddenly appeared or slowly grown through centuries without some protestation against the falsehood. We are therefore justified in assenting to the truth of a fact which is attested by tradition: the argument is considered good even in respect to moral obligations.

History must be authentic, true and entire. The authenticity of a book may be established by oral and written tradition, and also by an examination of the book itself. A book is authentic when its style is the same as the style of other books known to be by the same author, and when the contents of the book are in harmony with the known views, doctrines and opinions of the author. An historical work is true when the facts related, whether contemporaneous or past, are of great importance, are public in their nature, and are not contradicted by any historian of the same period. A history is known to be entire, when a comparison with the original manuscripts, or the first printed editions, shows no omission or alteration of statements in regard to important circumstances. When such a comparison cannot be made, we may judge by the unity of style and plan, and the satisfactory connection of events, that the work is entire.

In regard to monuments, it is necessary that they should have a necessary connection with the events commemorated, whether erected at the same time or afterwards.

It is objected that a certitude cannot be perfect which is diminishing gradually by the lapse of time and the loss of titles, which rests upon the testimony of witnesses less trustworthy than eye-witnesses, which becomes less clear as the date of the facts becomes more remote, and which, finally, has often been the source of deception. We answer, that a certitude once established is always a certitude; and though it may not afterwards affect our sensibilities so deeply, nevertheless its intrinsic nature is not thereby changed, and we always have sufficient means to detect a falsification when this takes place.

§ II. Authority of the testimony of men concerning supernatural facts.

A *supernatural fact* differs from a natural fact only with reference to the cause and the manner of its production. In regard to the effect, or the fact itself, it is a natural one. With this explanation, we proceed to demonstrate the following

Proposition.—*The testimony of men is an infallible motive of judging of supernatural facts.*

The truth of supernatural facts may be established by the testimony of men, provided this testimony has the same force for proving such facts, that it has for proving natural facts. But such is the case; for, as we said in the introduction to this proposition, and this assertion is denied by no one, a supernatural fact, in regard to its effect and exterior motive, is only a natural fact, and consequently can be established by similar proof, so that we might here repeat the argument already given in regard to natural facts. The testimony of men is true, when many witnesses relate the same fact, whether this be a miracle or a mere natural fact, provided it be evident that these witnesses have not been deceived and have not deceived. Hence the testimony of men is an infallible motive, &c.

The objections to this proposition rest upon the following assertion: A miracle is impossible. In this assertion there is an implied contradiction; for to pretend that all the witnesses to the miracles of our Lord were deceived or did deceive, is to assert a miracle in the moral order greater than the facts which are denied.

From what has been said, we may understand what is meant by *authority:* It is the motive by which we judge of those things which we do not know ourselves. Authority is human when it is the source of human faith or belief, and divine when our adhesion to it constitutes divine or supernatural faith.

Sixth Motive.—Memory.

Memory is that faculty by which we recall to mind feelings that are past.

Proposition.—Memory is an infallible motive of judging of a past state of the mind of which we have a clear recollection.

This proposition cannot be proved: it can only be explained.

I. There is certitude where there is a clear perception of a truth; but by memory, when our recollection is distinct, we have such a perception. Hence we have certitude.

II. Judgments based upon a universal, constant and irresistible propensity are infallible. This is admitted by every one; and were it not true we might doubt of everything, even of God himself. But by memory we form Judgments which are based upon an irresistible, constant and universal propensity; these judgments are therefore infallible. Hence memory is an infallible motive, &c.

Memory, like consciousness, produces an immediate certitude, and consequently cannot be demonstrated, since the demonstration should rest on memory itself. It is, in fact, by memory that we call to mind the very first principles, the bases, of every demonstration.

SEVENTH MOTIVE.—INDUCTION OR ANALOGY.

We reason by *induction* when we pass from phenomena observed and known to phenomena which are neither known nor observed. The following definition of induction may therefore be given: Induction is the operation by which, from several particular phenomena, the mind concludes the existence of a general law of nature.

The principle of induction rests upon the laws of nature. These laws may be summed up in these three axioms: 1st. There exists a constant and general order in the things which have been created, that is, in nature; 2nd. Every natural cause follows a certain order in the production of its effects; 3d. The same natural cause, placed in the same circumstances, produces the same effect.

We may now proceed to establish the following proposition concerning the principle of induction.

Proposition.—*A persuasion of the constancy and generality of the laws of nature is an infallible motive of certitude.*

What is born with us must be in harmony with the truth, and consequently an infallible motive of certitude; for if a persuasion natural to our mind could be false, the very constitution of the mind itself would be false, which would be the destruction of all certitude. But a persuasion of the constancy and generality of the laws of nature is innate; for it is universal, irresistible, and anterior to reason itself, as we see in the case of children, who instinctively avoid what is hurtful; such a persuasion is therefore an infallible motive of certitude.

We have seen, from the exposition of the principles of induction, that there are in nature general laws; but is it possible to have a true certitude in regard to the existence of the laws of nature in particular? In order to solve this question we proceed to establish this

Proposition.—*Induction sometimes gives true certitude concerning the laws of nature in particular.*

We have true certitude when we clearly perceive some truth, and when we may affirm it without any fear of erring. But by induction we know surely, and consequently perceive clearly, the existence of some laws of nature in particular; for instance, that fire will burn wood, melt lead, &c.; and we affirm the existence of these laws without any fear of erring. Certitude, then, sometimes gives us true certitude, &c.

Notes.—Induction gives certitude concerning the existence of a law of nature in particular, when there is some identity of circumstances in the phenomena which are observed, and this identity may be discovered by an attentive observation.

The certitude of facts known by induction is sometimes merely conditional and sometimes absolute.

The laws of nature, considered individually, are contingent, and God can suspend them when this suspension is not in opposition to his attributes, but not when such suspension would be in contradiction to any of these attributes. For instance, He could not cause a multitude of persons to agree among themselves to tell an untruth which would be injurious to their own interests. From this explanation, we may know when the certitude given by induction is conditional, and when it is absolute.

The laws of nature are two-fold, physical and psychological; the former governing corporal bodies, and the latter regulating spiritual substances. Moral laws are included in the psychological laws. By induction, we may learn the existence of psychological as well as of physical laws.

APPENDIX.—PROBABILITY.

Although, in itself, certitude is complete and

indivisible, yet it sometimes happens that a proposition true in itself, appears to us to approach the truth more or less nearly, according as we have more or less reason for believing it to be true. Those reasons which leave our minds in a state of uncertainty are called probabilities. When the probabilities in favor of a proposition are equal to those against it, we have what is called *doubt;* and when those in favor are more numerous than those against we have *verisimilitude*. *Probability*, then, is the motive which inclines us, in a greater or less degree, to believe as true that which is not completely demonstrated. As it is often very difficult to determine the degree of probability in favor of or against a given proposition, we must be cautious and not judge beyond what we perceive.

We admit historical facts which are only probable, whenever we have to doubt on account of the difficulty of criticising the sources of the history. In our daily actions, also, we often have to conduct ourselves according to information which is only probable. The further elucidation of this question belongs to theology.

In many questions relating to future events the issue depends upon a certain number of unknown possibilities: the probability of one of these possibilities may therefore be determined mathematically, and upon the result obtained, certain calculations may be based. In this manner contracts of insurance are drawn up, certain games of chance are predicted, &c. But evidently logic has nothing further to do with this subject. Here, then, closes the First Part of this work.

PART II.

METAPHYSICS.

METAPHYSICS.

METAPHYSICS literally means *above nature,* and "nature" here signifies the material world. The following definition of metaphysics is generally accepted: The science of supersensible and merely speculative things, as known to us by reason. By the words "merely speculative" metaphysics is distinguished from the other parts of philosophy.

Metaphysics is divided into two parts, general and special. General metaphysics has been called *ontology,* or the science of being; and special metaphysics has been called *pneumatology,* or the science of spiritual substances.

Pneumatology is divided into two parts, the first treating of God and His attributes, and the second of the human soul, its faculties and qualities. The first is called *theodicy,* or the science of God, and the second *psychology,* or a dissertation on the soul.

This order in the division of pneumatology is manifestly the proper one, for the knowledge of God and of his attributes is necessary in order to treat of various questions concerning the human soul. The destination of the soul for another life, for instance, cannot be proved until we have demonstrated the existence of God and his providence with his infinite wisdom and justice, ready after this life to render to every one according to his deserts.

FIRST DISSERTATION.

ON ONTOLOGY.

The word ontology comes from two Greek words, λόγος and ὤν, which together signify "discourse on being." Ontology may therefore be defined to be that part of philosophy which treats of being in general, and of the general species and relations of being. In this dissertation we consider being as abstracted from existence; and as we may have a positive idea of being thus abstractly considered, the title of this dissertation, "Ontology," or being in general, is correct.

We shall divide the subject of ontology into five chapters, treating in the first of the notion, essence and possibility of a being in general, in the second of its causes and its effects, in the third of its species, in the fourth of its properties, and in the fifth of space and duration.

CHAPTER FIRST.

Of the Notion, Essence and Possibility of a Being in General.

A *being* is that which exists or may exist. The notion of being is the first of all notions. We cannot think of anything unless there be some being;

hence the notion of being is logically prior to our thought, the notion of being is necessarily involved in thought.

The *essence* of a being is that without which a being can neither be nor be conceived to be. For instance, we cannot conceive the idea of a man without the notions or attributes of intelligence and animality.

The agreement among the essential attributes of a being forms the possibility of its existence. Consequently if certain attributes involve a contradiction they cannot constitute a being—that being is not possible. There is such a contradiction in a round square, consequently a round square is an impossibility.

The possibility, as we understand it here, abstracting it from the idea of existence, is what the philosophers call metaphysical or intrinsic possibility.

This accord among the essential attributes, which constitutes the possibility is immutable, and consequently necessary. It is immutable, for if it could be changed there would be, at the same time, accord and discord among the essential attributes of a being; that is, the same thing would at the same time both *be* and *not be*, which involves a contradiction and which is therefore absurd. That accord is then necessary since it is immutable: hence that accord, which is the essence or possibility of a being in general, does not depend on the free will of God; but since it is immutable and necessary, like God, it has its seat or foundation in God Himself, in the divine intellect, in the very essence of God. Descartes therefore was mistaken when he said the contrary.

Possibility of itself is not a sufficient reason for existence; that is, from the fact that a being is possible we cannot conclude that it exists. Existence is more than mere possibility; and if mere possibility were a sufficient reason for existence the effect would be greater than the cause, what is *plus* would be contained in what is *minus;* but this would involve a contradiction.

It follows, that since mere possibility is not a sufficient reason for existence, some existence must have existed before any possibility: hence, from this notion we deduce the idea of an eternal, necessary and infinite being.

The essential attributes of a being, or its essence, either metaphysical or physical, constitutes the nature of that being. The word nature, however, has a greater extension than the word essence; it comprehends not only the attributes which are essential, but also what flows from them. Hence, those attributes are essential without which a being can neither be nor be conceived to be; and those attributes are natural which are formed in a being by the force of its essence. For instance, the roots, the trunk and the branches are the essential parts of a tree; but its bulk, height, &c., are its natural parts.

Two axioms are drawn from the considerations made in this chapter, with regard to essence:

1st. What is, is; or, negatively, the same thing cannot *be* and *not be* at the same time. This is generally called the principle of contradiction.

2nd. Whatever is involved in a being must be

affirmed of its essence; and whatever is excluded from a being must be denied of its essence.

CHAPTER SECOND.

OF THE CAUSES AND THE EFFECTS OF BEINGS.

Let us first establish the difference which exists between principle and cause. *Principle* is that which contains the reason for the existence of something. Our mind, for instance, is the principle of our thoughts; that is, our thoughts could not come from a substance different in its nature from our mind: in other words, the substance from which thought flows is spiritual and active.

When the principle contains the whole reason for the possibility or the existence of a being it is called *adequate*, if the principle does not contain the whole reason it is called *inadequate*. The adequate principle is also called the *sufficient reason*.

Cause is that which produces something, or which concurs in the production of something. Hence there are two kinds of causes. The first is called the *efficient cause;* and this only, properly speaking, is a real cause, for only this produces an effect. The other concurs in the production of the effect, and is only improperly called a cause.

This last, or incomplete, cause may be *material, formal, instrumental, final,* or *exemplary,* according as we consider the material, the form, the instrument, the end, or the model which has been used by the agent.

The efficient cause is either necessary or free.

The cause is *necessary* when it necessarily produces its effects, and it is *free* when it may either produce them or not produce them. The human mind, in regard to its free determinations, is a free cause.

The efficient cause may also be either a first cause or a secondary cause. It is a *first cause* when it does not depend upon another cause in order to act, and a *secondary cause* when it does depend on another cause in order to act.

The efficient cause is also either physical or moral; *physical*, when it produces an effect which belongs to the physical order; and *moral*, when the effect is a moral one. The man who orders another to commit a murder is the moral cause of the death which he has ordered. The physical cause is also called the *direct* cause, and the moral cause the *indirect* cause.

The efficient cause is moreover either *general* or *particular*, which words are readily understood; and also either actual or virtual; *actual*, if we consider the effect produced, and *virtual*, if we consider the power of producing it as residing in the cause.

The efficient cause is, finally, a cause *per se*, when it produces the effect which it aims at; and a cause *per accidens*, when the effect produced is not the one intended, but an accidental one.

NOTE.—There is a difference between the cause and the condition. The *condition* is the difficulty to be conquered in order to obtain the effect. It is consequently the way of producing the effect.

An intelligent cause does not act without aiming

at some end: the *end*, then, is that which involves the reason why an action is undertaken; it has been improperly called the *final cause*.

The end may be either *primary* or *secondary*, *proximate* or *remote*, *intermediate* or *final*. The end is *intermediate* when it is connected with two others, one preceding and the other following; and it is *final* when the agent, after having obtained it, is at rest, that is, has accomplished his purpose.

The *means* (media) are everything instrumental in the production of an effect. These means must be in proportion to the cause that uses them, and to the end which is aimed at. Some of them are necessary, and others only useful.

Order, in general, is the regular arrangement of causes, means and ends. When we consider that arrangement in reference to the essence of things, we have the *metaphysical order;* when we consider it in reference to the existence of bodies, we have the *physical order;* and when we consider the same arrangement in reference to the free actions of God, of the angels, or of the souls of men, we have the *moral order*.

The moral order is called *religious* when it refers to the worship of God, *social* when it regulates the intercourse of men with one another, and *political* when its object embraces the correlative duties of the State and its citizens.

The metaphysical order is the foundation of the other two. In the whole universality of things there exists a perfect subordination of causes, means and effects, so that all possible and existing beings are perfectly chained together.

This three-fold order being the object of science, it follows that science is metaphysical, physical and moral: and as everything which is known, or which may be known, by reason only, forms the object of philosophy, and everything which is made manifest to us by divine revelation constitutes the object of theology, it appears further that the order of science is double, natural and supernatural.

From what has been explained in this chapter we may deduce the following axioms:

I. He who wills the end wills the means.
II. The means must be in proportion to the end.
III. There is no effect without a cause.
IV. The cause is prior to the effect.
V. The perfections of the effect cannot be greater than those of the cause.

If a perfection in the effect could exceed the perfection in the cause, that perfection would be without a cause, which is absurd.

The cause may contain its effect in a three-fold manner:

1st. Formally,—as a heap of gold contains formally, or according to their nature and forms, several particles of the same metal.

2d. Virtually,—as the architect has in his mind the plan of the building which he is to erect.

3d. Eminently,—as when the cause contains all the perfections of the effect, in a most eminent manner and one quite unknown to us. God has in himself, in a most eminent manner, all the perfections of his creatures.

The following corollaries result from the axioms given above:

I. No being can be its own cause; for, if so, it would, at the same time, be prior and posterior to itself.

II. Two beings cannot be mutually their own cause.

CHAPTER THIRD.

Of the Different Species of Being.

1st. A being exists either in itself or in another being: in the first case we have what is called *substance*, in the second *modification*.

2nd. A being is either finite or infinite.

3d. A being is either material or spiritual.

Hence the division of this chapter into three articles.

Article First.—Substance and Modification.

A *substance* is a being existing in itself: this does not mean that such a being is independent of a cause, but only that it is independent of another substance as an object in which it should lie in order to exist; thus, a stone is a substance, for it does not need another being to which it must be attached in order to exist.

A *modification* is that which needs another being to which it may adhere in order to exist, as color. Modification is also called accident; it is the substance appearing to us with such or such determined form. Hence the modification is not something of a positive being added to the substance; but it is the substance itself determined in such or such manner. The following axiom is clear of itself: "Modification supposes substance." It follows from the foregoing definitions that modification cannot exist without substance, nor substance without modification; and that the modification, materially speaking, or considered in a material point of view is perceived before the substance.

Substance is created or not created, and complete or not complete.

A *complete* substance is a substance *sui juris* (of its own right), that is, one which is not united to another substance in order to be perfect, and which, consequently, is the principle of its own operations, if it has any. Peter is a complete substance. A complete substance is also called a *suppositum*.

A substance is *incomplete* when it is united to another substance in order to be perfect, as the body by itself, the soul by itself.

There is a difference between a substance and a *suppositum*. A *suppositum* is always a substance, but a substance is not always a *suppositum*.

When the *suppositum* is endowed with reason it becomes a *person*.

When a person is composed of several substances, united in order to constitute it, we have the hypostasis, or hypostatic union.

From what has been said, we deduce the following axioms:

I. Actions are personal; that is, actions ought not

to be attributed to each or any substance composing a person, but to the union of all, or the person itself.

II. Actions share the dignity of the person acting. Hence the actions of our Lord were of an infinite value.

III. Names belong to the persons or *suppositums*.

ARTICLE SECOND.—INFINITE AND FINITE SUBSTANCES.

Substance is infinite or finite.

Infinite substance is that having no limitation. It is the same as simple being, or absolute being (*ens simpliciter*).

Finite substance is that which is limited.

Some authors divide the infinite into the infinite *actu*, or the actual infinite, that which is the highest and most perfect that can be imagined, namely, God alone; and the infinite *potentia*, or the potential or virtual infinite, which can be infinitely increased or diminished. But certainly this division cannot be accepted; since the infinite, and a substance which can be increased, are two terms involving a contradiction. That which is infinite is so of its own nature, and can therefore be neither increased nor diminished. The infinite absolutely excludes limitation; hence it is immutable. The so-called virtual infinite should be called the *indefinite*.

We shall see farther on, that the infinite being is the same as the *necessary being*, and the finite being the same as the *contingent being*.

That we have in our mind the idea of the infinite is certain, for we can define it, and it is in our mind distinct from any other idea. This idea, according to Descartes, Mallebranche, Leibnitz and Bossuet, in opposition to Locke and the other sensists, is a positive idea, but not an adequate, though a true and clear one. Evidently it has been placed in our mind by God himself, since the finite could not give the idea of the infinite: no one can give what he has not himself.

The idea of a finite being, considered materially, that is, as having a real existence, is also a positive idea; but considered formally, that is, as deprived of some reality which it might possess but does not, is a negative idea.

Article Third.—Material and Spiritual Substances.

Substance is, again, either material or spiritual.

A *material being* is one which is essentially extensive and inert; and a *spiritual being* is one which is essentially active and thinking. There is consequently a fundamental difference between these two beings.

Matter is essentially divisible, since it is extensive; but whether matter is infinitely divisible, and what are the elements of matter, have been questions of dispute.

The opinion of Descartes and his followers is that matter is infinitely divisible; for, they say, since extension belongs to the essence of matter, as long as you have matter you have extension, and consequently divisibility. In their view, a simple element becoming extensive by aggregation involves a contradiction.

On the other hand, Leibnitz and his disciples are of opinion that the *monads*, which is the name given by them to the elements of matter, are simple beings; an infinite divisibility, in their view, involving a contradiction. Any composite being, they teach, is formed of composing elements; but with the system of Descartes we should have a composite substance without composing elements.

In both these systems we find at least apparent contradictions. According to the system of Descartes, the infinite is contained in the finite; while, according to the system of Leibnitz, a substance, or a simple *monad*, which is essentially unextensive, becomes extensive by aggregation.

It is morally impossible to give a satisfactory solution of these questions: still, the system of Leibnitz seems, in general, to be more acceptable than that of Descartes.

Spiritual substance is quadruple; namely, God, the Angels, the human soul and the soul of the beasts.

Material substance is multiple, as may be seen in the study of Natural Philosophy.

CHAPTER FOURTH.

Of the Properties of Being.

The *properties* of a being are those parts which constitute the being; they are so called because they are its own *proper* parts (propria).

I. Some properties are common to all beings, considered in themselves; these are: Unity, truth and goodness. Every being must be one, true and good.

First, *unity*. No positive definition can be given of the unity commonly called numerical, but by the philosophers metaphysical.

The following negative definition of unity is given by the scholastics: One is that which is divided, that is distinct, from every other being, but undivided in itself.

The metaphysical unity is found in every being; for every being must be undivided. If a being could be divided into several parts, each part would be a separate being, and there would be several beings instead of one. On the other hand, it is clear that every being must be distinct from every other.

This numerical or metaphysical unity may be:

1st. *Substantial Unity*, or simplicity, which belongs to substances that cannot be divided, because they exclude composition of parts. Such is the unity of the soul, or of any of the spirits.

2nd. *Physical Unity*, which is composed of parts united by some physical bond. Such is the unity of the human body.

3d. *Moral unity*, which is composed of parts united by a moral tie, as the unity of a family.

Second, *truth*. A being is true when it agrees with its own attributes. The truth of a being is its conformity with its own archetype, that is, with the idea of that being as it exists in the divine intellect. This truth, which is the metaphysical truth, is found in all beings, even those which are merely possible.

Truth is also either moral or logical, according as it refers to beings which belong to the moral or to the logical order.

Third, *goodness.* Goodness is the aptitude of a being to attain its own ends. It is clear that this property is found in all beings, since God is infinitely wise.

This definition is of metaphysical or absolute goodness. Moral goodness is a property of reasonable and free beings.

Goodness does not pertain to bad actions; for a bad action, or a sin, is something merely negative. A bad action is an action lacking in righteousness; but the lack or absence of righteousness is nothing positive, nor is it any being, but the negative of being and of perfection.

II. Some properties are merely relative; that is, they pertain to beings when compared with other beings. All beings are in continual relations with one another. We may define *relation*, in general, to be a property pertaining to a being when compared with another being. In a relation, considered in general, there are three elements, a subject, a term and a foundation. If, for instance, I compare the whiteness of paper with that of snow, the paper is the subject, the snow is the term to which I refer the subject, and whiteness is the foundation or the reason for referring the first element to the second. The term and the subject are the correlatives.

These elements are essential, or natural; or they are arbitrary, or accidental. They are *essential* when they flow from the very essence of things, as the relations between a cause and its effects. They are *arbitrary* when they are grounded on the mere opinions of men. Such are all the symbolical objects, in relation to the moral beings which they signify, as the relation between the olive branch and peace; and also all the moral relations, as that existing between a king and his subjects.

Among the relations are classed identity and distinction.

Identity may be taken in several senses, but here it is the perseverance of a being in the same state. This identity may be physical or moral. Living beings have a moral identity, not a metaphysical or absolute one.

The identity of the human soul is not an accidental one; that is, it is not an identity consisting in the maintainance of the similitude of modifications, but is a substantial identity.

Individuals endowed with reason retain their personal identity so long as they maintain their subsistence and rationality.

Distinction is the negative of identity. There is a difference between distinction and diversity. What is diverse is distinct; but that which is distinct is not always diverse. Heaven and earth are distinct and diverse; Peter and Paul are distinct, but not diverse. Distinction excludes identity, and diversity excludes similitude.

Two beings entirely alike may exist, for their existence involves no contradiction.

CHAPTER FIFTH.

Of Space and Time.

Space, in general, is extension, in which bodies exist, or in which they may exist or be conceived as possible. Hence the division of space into *real space*, in which bodies actually exist, and *abstract space*, in which they are conceived as possible. Abstract space is the object of geometry.

The conception of abstract space is formed in our minds by abstraction in the same manner as we form all our conceptions of possible beings. For instance, when we see many bodies having among themselves relations of situation and position, our minds may abstract, or remove, every other property pertaining to these bodies, even their actual existence, and consider that sole property by which they may occupy various positions with regard to one another, then we have the idea of an abstract extension, or of abstract space.

Space, conceived abstractly, is eternal, necessary and immutable, in the same manner as we conceive as eternal, necessary and immutable all possible beings. Space is virtually (potentia) infinite, using the word "infinite," as we have before explained, in the sense of indefinite. It is also immense and indefinitely divisible.

A *place* is a determined part or point of space.

Time is the duration of a being, or the permanence of its existence. Time is also defined to be the duration in which contingent beings succeed each other, or may continue those successions. Time also, we may observe, is, like space, real and abstract.

Time is divided, first, into past, present and future, and, second, into real and abstract time, all of which words are sufficiently clear.

Eternity, properly so called, is duration without a beginning or an end; and eternity, improperly so called, is duration without an end, but with a beginning: this last is the same as immortality, and by the scholastics is called eternity *a parte post*. As succession requires a first point, eternity, properly so called, has no succession, for it has no beginning. Consequently the idea of time as lasting from all eternity involves a contradiction; hence, the eternal being does not exist in time, because this being does not admit of succession. We may say, however, that the eternal being in its immutable duration co-exists with the successive mutations of contingent beings.

There have been many opinions expressed by the learned concerning the nature of space and time, the two main ones being those of Clarke and Leibnitz.

Clarke, whose opinion was accepted by Newton, taught that what he called absolute or abstract space and time are nothing else than the immensity and the eternity of God. This opinion is not acceptable for the following reasons:

1st. We do not conceive abstract space and abstract time as things actually infinite, but only virtually so, that is, as things always admitting of increase; while, at the same time, we conceive the eternity and the immensity of God as two attributes actually infinite, and we cannot conceive them differently. Consequently the notions of space and time, as we conceive them, are contradictory to the notion of the infinite.

2nd. We do not conceive abstract space and abstract time as things really and individually existing, but as two abstractions of the mind; while eternity and immensity exist really and individually in God, although they cannot be separated from the divine substance.

3d. It is evident that the opinion of Clarke much favors pantheism; for since, as we have seen, space and time are not actually infinite, but only virtually so, which is the same as indefinite or finite with no determined limits, it follows that if space and time may be considered as attributes of the divine substance, nothing can prevent us from considering the other finite beings also as attributes of God.

Leibnitz teaches that space and time are not beings distinct from the other contingent beings, but that they are mere relations of those beings, space being the relation of situation among bodies, and time the relation of succession among contingent beings. Consequently, if there were no contingent beings there would be neither space nor time; and when contingent beings began to exist then also began the existence of space and time.

This explanation seems true, and gives full satisfaction to the mind. But Leibnitz mingles with this part of his doctrine some notions concerning the extension of matter, taken from his system of monads, which do not seem so satisfactory. Omitting these notions, we may accept the explanation given above.

Epicurus, Democritus, and several among the moderns, make space to be a substantial being which is infinite and contains all bodies. Descartes does not admit of abstract space, but teaches that space is a material and substantial being.

Kant, who denies the objectivity of bodies, applies his system to this question. His idealism has been indirectly refuted in Logic, where we established the truth that the evidence of the senses is an infallible motive of certitude.

SECOND DISSERTATION.

ON THEODICY.

This subject is naturally divided into two parts, in the first of which we treat of the existence of God, and in the second of his attributes.

PART FIRST.—THE EXISTENCE OF GOD.

Some men do not admit the existence of God, and these are called *Atheists*, a name derived from the Greek (α θεος, no God). We may consequently call those who believe in the existence of God *theists*. This first part is therefore naturally subdivided into two chapters.

CHAPTER FIRST.

Of Atheism.

Atheists are either *speculative* or *practical* disbelievers in the existence of God: the former do not acknowledge his existence; the latter know that he exists, but live as if they did not know it. Speculative atheists are called *negative* when they simply deny the existence of God, and *positive* when they attempt to prove that he does not exist: the positive atheists are also called *systematic* atheists.

Note.—There is a difference between theism and deism, although the two words have substantially the same etymology. *Theism* is the doctrine of those who believe in God and in his operations; while *Deism* is the doctrine of those who also believe in God, but entirely reject divine revelation.

The causes of atheism proceed from the intellect or from the will; being in the first case (a) an imperfect knowledge, or (b) an abuse of certain sciences; and in the second (a) corruption, or (b) pride.

§ 1. Is it prudent to remain indifferent concerning the existence of God?

Such indifference is certainly very unwise; for it is a question upon which depends our greatest happiness or our greatest misery.

The atheists reason in this manner: "I do not know who placed me in this world; nor do I know what the world is, or even what I am myself. I do not know what my body is, or my senses, or my soul, or this part of me which thinks of what I am now saying. I see those frightful spaces of the universe which surround me, and I find myself fixed on a speck of this immensity, not knowing why I have been placed here rather than elsewhere; nor why the small space of time which I have to live has been assigned to me at this moment rather than at any other moment of eternity. I see immensities everywhere; they engulf me as an atom, or as a shadow that lasts but for an instant. All that I know is that I shall soon die; and yet that which I try most to forget is this very death which I cannot avoid. As I do not know where I came from, so I do not know where I am going to; I know only that, leaving this world, I fall forever into nothingness, or else into the hands of an angry God: and not knowing which of these alternatives will be my lot, I conclude that it is better for me to pass my life without thinking of what shall happen to me; and believe that I have but to follow my inclinations without reflection or anxiety concerning what ought or ought not to be done in order not to fall into eternal damnation, in case that what is said of this be true. Perhaps I might find some light to dissipate my doubts, but I do not wish to take any trouble about the matter, nor do I care to make one step to find this light; and so, looking with contempt on those who trouble themselves with such cares, I prefer to go on, and wait without fear for that great event, allowing myself to be carried on quietly to death in the uncertainty of my future condition." Such are the horrible sentiments of the Atheist.

The chief argument of the Atheists is an evident

absurdity. They say: If God exists he is infinitely good, consequently there is nothing to be feared. They forget that God is also infinitely just.

§ 2. Are there any evils resulting from the adoption of the theory of the Atheists?

This system is the source of many evils to men, whether considered individually or collectively, that is, as members of society.

1st. Atheism is hurtful to men considered as individuals; for it takes away from them all security, all comfort in misfortune, and every hope of happiness. It takes away all security; for in all the labors of life, what gives us courage is the consideration that God will bless our efforts for own welfare and for that of those dependent upon us. It takes away all consolation and hope, and consequently stifles the voice of nature to which the pagans themselves gave ear. We find no real happiness in this world, because here every good is mingled with sorrow and of short duration, because many suffer constantly, and because the thought of death disturbs our joys. Hence Atheism, which takes away the hope of a better world, is hurtful to man, considered individually.

2d. Atheism is also hurtful to men considered as members of society, for (a) it leaves authority without restraint. (Authority cannot be judged, condemned and punished by its own subjects). And (b) it leaves the citizen without morals. (Whence would come restraint against vice, if Atheism prevailed? Without God there would be no other life, nor would conscience exist, nor would the laws have any sanction).

Atheism breaks every bond of union among men. Those bonds are the virtues: gratitude, deference, obedience, sincerity, justice, &c., and without God there would be no virtue.

§ 3. Is theism better than atheism? The observations made above are sufficient to give an affirmative answer to this question.

§ 4. Is theism safer than atheism?

A doctrine in which there is nothing to be dreaded, if false, and everything to be hoped, if true, is safer than one in which there is nothing to be hoped for, if true, and much to be dreaded, if false. But such is the case in regard to this question; hence theism is safer than atheism.

§ 5. Is atheism worse than polytheism?

That doctrine is the worse which restrains our passions the less. Atheism restrains our passions less than polytheism; for polytheism admits the belief in another life. Consequently, atheism is worse than polytheism.

It is objected to this, that without God, 1st, there would be the natural law; 2nd, that religion has been the cause of many wars; 3d, that many atheists have been good men, while many theists have been bad men; 4th, that the atheist is inclined to do evil by his nature only, while the polytheist is inclined to evil both by his nature and by the example of his gods; and 5th, that it is better to deny God than to attribute to him vices which debase him.

We answer, to the 1st, that without God there would be no sanction to the natural law, and without a sanction no law can have force; to the 2nd, that religion has been the pretext, but not the cause of war (We may here observe that we speak of religion as being the aggressive power; for religion has often been obliged to defend herself. The cause of these wars was ambition, or a spirit of revenge on the part of princes who were censured by the popes, or some other cause of similar nature); to the 3d, that neither theists nor atheists were logical in their conduct, and that therefore no conclusion can be drawn from their conduct, to deduce a general conclusion from exceptional facts is a fallacy *per accidens;* to the 4th, that the polytheists have some motives for restraining their passions, for example, the belief in another life; and to the 5th, that the ignorance of the polytheists is not the result of a bad will, that consequently their intentions are good, and that since the intention constitutes the merit or the demerit of our actions, the conduct of the atheists is worse than that of the polytheists.

CHAPTER SECOND.

Of the Proofs of the Existence of God.

No truth has been more firmly established than that of the existence of God. The arguments by which this truth is proved are of three kinds, being taken respectively from the metaphysical, the physical and the moral order; and consequently the present chapter is divided into three articles.

Article First.—Metaphysical Arguments.

These arguments are so called because they are

grounded upon the essence of things, and are drawn from considerations purely intellectual.

Some preliminary notions more fully explained in Ontology must be summarily repeated in this connection:

No being exists without a reason for its existence. This reason may come from the nature of the being, or from a cause which is extrinsic to it. A being which has in its own nature the reason of its existence, or which exists by itself out of its own nature, is called a *necessary being*, or a being *a se*. The opposite of a necessary being is called a *contingent being*, that is, a being which has received its existence from an extrinsic cause.

An *infinite being* is one which admits of no limit; it is also called *ens simpliciter*, because it excludes negation in every way. The notion of infinite necessarily excludes that of number or series: the idea of an infinite number or series is contradictory in itself.

First argument, taken from the notion of a necessary being.

Proposition.—*From the existence of a necessary being we conclude that God exists.*

Argument: God exists if there is a necessary being; but such is the case; therefore God exists.

Proof: There is a necessary being. For, among the beings now existing, either there is a necessary being or all beings are contingent. But this latter supposition cannot be true; for, if all existing beings are contingent they must have received their existence from another being: but it cannot be that all existing beings have received their existence, for, if they had, they must have received it from a being taken either outside or inside the collection of existing beings: but neither of these suppositions can be true; for, since none but contingent beings exist, the being upon which they depend cannot be taken outside of them; and it cannot be taken from inside their collection, for then it would be both contingent and non-contingent; it would be cause and effect, prior and posterior to itself, which is a contradiction: there must therefore be a being which is not contingent, that is, a necessary being.

Conclusion.—The necessary being is infinite. It is infinite if it has all the perfections, existing or possible, of all existing or possible beings; but such is the case: for all contingent beings come from the necessary being; but perfections are modifications of beings; hence, all perfections existing in contingent beings come from the necessary being: this necessary being must have all possible perfections also, for otherwise these perfections would be possible and not possible at the same time. Therefore the necessary being is the infinite, and the infinite is God.

Second argument, taken from the idea of God.

Proposition.—*From the idea of God we conclude that God exists.*

Argument: From the idea of God we conclude that God exists, if we have really that idea, and if that idea is necessarily connected with the actual existence of God. But such is the case; hence, from the idea of God we conclude that God exists.

Proof: 1st. We have the idea of God, that is, of a being infinitely perfect: this idea is clear in our mind, and distinct from any other notion.

2nd. The actual existence of God is necessarily connected with the idea of God; for if not we might conceive him as possible only, but we cannot conceive God as merely possible. We cannot conceive a being without its essence; the essence of God is to be: we cannot therefore conceive God except as actually existing. Hence, the idea which we have of God is necessarily connected with the existence of God; and, consequently, from the idea of God we conclude that God exists.

Third argument, taken from the idea of the infinite.

Proposition.—*From the idea of the infinite we conclude that God exists.*

Argument: The infinite exists, and consequently God exists, if we have the idea of the infinite; but such is the case; hence, from the idea of the infinite we conclude that God exists.

Proof: The idea of the infinite involves the existence of the infinite, since this idea can come but from the infinite itself.

1st. The idea of the infinite cannot be given to us by a finite being; for, if so, we should have an effect greater than its cause, which involves a contradiction.

2nd. No one can give what he has not; hence, the idea of the infinite comes from the infinite itself.

We have the idea of the infinite; for, as in the case of the idea of God, we perceive it; it is clear and distinct in our mind. Hence, the idea of the infinite involves the existence of the infinite, and consequently, the existence of God.

Article Second.—Physical Argument.

The physical argument is taken from the aspect of the universe, and the beautiful order found therein. The Atheists pretend that the world was made by chance, and Epicurus embodied this system in the following manner: From all eternity an immense vacuum existed, and in this vacuum matter was found to have existed from all eternity. This matter was not found collected in one mass, but divided into its primitive atoms. To these atoms Epicurus gives the following properties: They had various forms; they were eternal and necessary; they were indivisible on account of their extreme hardness; they moved in the vacuum in straight lines. It happened that some of these atoms deviated from the straight lines and adhered to other atoms, thus forming various bodies, until gradually the world resulted from this disorder.

We may observe that these principles are quite arbitrary; and that, our definitions of the words necessary and infinite being accepted, these same principles are also absurd and contradictory. Besides, the consequences are false; for, from our definition of the necessary being, it follows, that the world has been created, and created by God; while, from the system of Epicurus, it follows, that the order of harmony, the conservation and reproduction of material beings, are merely the result of the deviations of atoms wandering in a vacuum, in which an infinite matter is found. Who does not smile at such incoherencies! It is needless to say more of this system. Let us come to our argument, and establish the following

Proposition.—*The order of the physical world indirectly proves the existence of God.*

Argument: This proposition is true provided there is order in the physical world, and that this order comes from a being of supreme intelligence; but such is the case, and consequently the order of the physical world proves the existence of God.

Proof.—A. Order is found in the physical world. The parts which constitute the physical world are the planetary and stellar systems, and the two-fold kingdom of nature, the inorganic and the organic. In the inorganic it will be sufficient to point out the atmosphere; while in the organic we have the vegetable and the animal creation. In all these we find a beautiful order; that is, the most suitable disposition of means for the end in view.

B. This order comes from a being of supreme intelligence. This assertion is true, provided (a) the author of this order is a being distinct from matter and endowed with intelligence; and provided (b) the cause of this order infinitely surpasses the human mind in intelligence. As both of these are true, it follows that this order comes from a being of supreme intelligence.

(a) That the cause is intelligent and distinct from matter appears from this; Order is a disposition of the means necessary to reach an end; consequently, the author of this order must be able to know both the end and the means necessary to reach it; it must then be an immaterial and intelligent cause, since matter is inert, blind and void of intelligence.

(b) This cause infinitely surpasses the human mind in intelligence. All admit that the order found in the works of nature is far superior to anything produced by the human mind. This order is so perfect that the human mind has never been able to discover all its perfections; new wonders are found every day, while many more escape the most ingenious researches. Hence it appears that this intelligent cause immeasurably surpasses the human mind, and therefore it must be God.

This argument destroys the system of Epicurus, since it proves that the order of the universe does not spring from chance, that is, from a blind cause; it also overturns the system of the Pantheists, who pretend that God is not distinct from matter: but it does not absolutely prove the existence of God, that is, it does not prove that the intelligence that formed the universe is infinite, but only that it immeasurably surpasses mere human intelligence.

NOTE.—From what has been said, we may conclude that matter is contingent and consequently that it has been created; hence, its existence proves that of a creator. Matter, we have further seen, is inert; and we may conceive it as existing without motion: hence, motion is not a necessary quality of matter, and as motion exists, we conclude that there has been a prime mover. These observations will supply the means of answering the objection raised against the creation from the axiom *ex nihilo nihil fit.* If "nihilo" here means a *cause*, the axiom is true; but if the axiom means that what was merely possible may not become actual, it is false.

Article Third.—Moral Argument.

A *moral proof* is one drawn from some fact that belongs to the moral nature of man; that is, a fact based on the propensities or opinions which are common to all men. Such proof produces in the mind a certitude not less than that resulting from metaphysical or physical proofs. Hence, the certitude resulting from a moral argument ought not to be confounded with what is called moral certitude, a term which often signifies nothing more than probability.

First argument, taken from the common consent of mankind.

Proposition.—*From the unanimous consent of mankind, it follows that God exists.*

Argument: If at all times and among all nations men have believed in the existence of God, we may conclude that God does exist. But there has always and among all nations been such a belief. Hence, the unanimous consent of mankind proves the existence of God.

Proof: The fact may be established as follows: we may know that all peoples have at all time believed in the existence of God, if we find everywhere and in all ages prayers, temples, altars, sacrifices and religious rites. But this fact is abundantly proved for ancient times by all the writers, sacred or profane, who deserve our confidence. The fact is as clearly evident for our own times, from the testimony of numberless travelers and writers. No nation, civilized and enlightened, or barbarous and savage, has been found where some form of worship could not be discovered.

This consent is universal, uniform, and constant, and no one denies that the fact to which it testifies is of the greatest importance; consequently this testimony has all the conditions required in the treatise on certitude to constitute an infallible motive of certitude. Therefore God exists.

This proof is complete, and allows us to conclude the existence of an infinite being; because such is the notion, although sometimes obscure, which is found in the minds of all people concerning God.

Second argument, taken from the existence of the natural law.

Proposition.—*The existence of the natural law proves the existence of God.*

Argument: God exists if there is a natural law, but there is a natural law, hence He exists.

Proof: The natural law is that rule, commanding what is right and forbidding what is wrong, which is found in the conscience of every man. Since it is found in all men, it is the voice of truth, that is, the voice of God. But there is no law without a legislator; and since the natural law is implanted in the hearts of all men the legislator must be prior to man and superior to him, that is God.

PART SECOND.—THE ATTRIBUTES OF GOD.

An *attribute* is a quality declared to belong to a being; and as perfection is an attribute which it is better to have than not to have, it follows that all the attributes of God are perfect; hence, to speak of the attributes of God is the same as to speak of his perfections.

Perfections are *absolute* when they exclude any limitation, and *relative* when they admit some limitation. The first are found in God alone, and the others in the creation; but God necessarily possesses all absolute perfections formally, that is, as they are, and all relative perfections *modo eminenti* in an eminent manner.

Concerning the question as to which is the primary attribute of God, we find four opinions. Some say that it is his unity, that is, his existence by himself. The Thomists contend that God is first an eminent and actual intelligence; while the Scotists declare that his primary attribute is his infinity; but in all these opinions we have conceptions of God considered in reference to the creation; these conceptions must consequently be posterior, logically speaking, to the conception of his being, or of his existence: the fourth opinion, therefore, according to which, logically speaking, the primary attribute of God is "to be simply," would seem to be more satisfactory.

The attributes of God are divided into two classes, relative and absolute. The relative attributes are those which are proper to each of the three persons of the Holy Trinity: the discussion of these belongs to theology. The absolute attributes are those which belong to the divine essence.

As we have said, God is a simple substance; the assertion of the contrary would involve a contradiction. The difficulty then is to explain these attributes of God. Is the distinction given above real, or logical, that is, virtual only? Is it real; that is, does there exist in God the same distinction of attributes as there exists in the human soul between the will and the intellect? or, is this distinction virtual only, that is, the result of the action or manifestation of God's attributes, appearing to us as if there was a real distinction in them?

The Scotists teach that there is a real distinction among God's attributes, and the Thomists affirm the contrary. The doctrine of the Thomists certainly offers less difficulty in reasoning on this mysterious question. St. Augustine, before St. Thomas, gave the second opinion as his own. "No," says he, "there is no real distinction among the attributes of God; but it is the essence of God which is, at the same time, most simple and most manifold, being a simple multiplicity and a multiple simplicity." It must be confessed that these antitheses do not throw any light on the subject.

We shall divide this question concerning the attributes of God into thirteen chapters; treating successively of his unity, his eternity, his immutability, his liberty, his independence and omnipotence, his simplicity, his immensity, his intelligence and knowledge, his wisdom, his sanctity and truth, his goodness and happiness, his justice, and his providence.

CHAPTER FIRST.

OF THE UNITY OF GOD.

This attribute of God has been denied by the Polytheists and by the Manicheans. The Polytheists admitted a plurality or multiplicity of gods, while the Manicheans affirmed that there are two principles of all things, one bad, who is the originator of all evil, and the other good, who is of course the cause of all good. In order to proceed methodically, let us divide the present chapter into three articles.

ARTICLE FIRST.—THE UNITY OF GOD PROVED AGAINST THE POLYTHEISTS.

The forms of Polytheism have been manifold; being denominated Demonolatry, or worship of demons, Anthropolatry, or worship of men, Herolatry, or worship of heroes, Zoolatry, or worship of animals, Idolatry, or worship of idols or statues, and Fetichism, or worship of objects having no determined form.

It is impossible to find out exactly when Polytheism made its first appearance in the world; but it is certain that it has never been general, that, besides the philosophers, the generality of the people had some idea, though a confused one, of the unity of God. It is certain, moreover, that Monotheism was prior to it, contrary to the teaching of some writers who pretend that Christianity is but a phase of Polytheism. It is clear also that Polytheism did not grow more perfect in the course of time, but it degenerated and engendered general corruption, placing the world on the verge of an abyss, so that, according to the opinion of Bossuet, the world would have relapsed into chaos again if Jesus Christ had not come to save it. It has been asked whether Polytheism sprang from the will or from the intellect. We may accept as the true opinion that Polytheism originated mainly from the corruption of the will.

Against the Polytheists we proceed to establish the following

Proposition.—*God is one.*

1st. We have shown that God is a necessary being, or a being simply, that is, one who has in himself the whole fullness of being, or existence. He cannot therefore be multiple; for if there were any being or a plenitude of being extrinsic to him it could not be said that he possesses the whole fullness of being.

2nd. The necessary being is infinite; that is, the necessary being excludes any limitation: hence he is one, otherwise there would be limitation.

3d. The unity of harmony which is found in the creation shows that its author and preserver is one.

4th. We may add to the above reasons the consent of nations; for it may be clearly demonstrated that the Pagans themselves admitted the unity of God.

Article Second.—The Unity of God Proved Against the Dualists.

We find among the Semitic races, especially in Egypt and Persia, a belief in the existence of two first principles, one the principle of matter, and the other the principle of spirit. This Dualism is not that which we propose to examine in this article, but rather that which was put forth by Manes in the second and third centuries of the Christian era, and revived by Bayle in the seventeenth century. These men taught that all evil comes from the bad principle and all good from the good principle; but their doctrine cannot be accepted, for,

1st. God is one—there cannot be two necessary beings. The necessary being is infinite; the infinite being contains the fullness of being or existence: he cannot therefore be multiple; and hence he is one.

2nd. Of these two beings one would be infinitely perfect and the other infinitely imperfect; but imperfection is a negation, that is nothing; hence the principle of evil would be infinitely nothing, which is an absurdity.

3d. Laying aside the former considerations, neither of these beings would be omnipotent, and neither would be happy, unless they made an agreement with each other concerning all things which should be done, and then we should have fatalism, that is, human liberty would be annihilated.

4th. In conclusion, we will say that this system is not necessary in order to explain any difficulties in the mechanism of the world.

Article Third.—The Origin of Evil Under a Being Infinitely Good.

It is true that it appears difficult to explain the origin of evil under a being infinitely good; still we cannot reject the unity of God on account of this, for that truth has been established.

Let us then make a few considerations concerning this question of the origin of evil. The evil in the world is three-fold.

1st. The evil which is called metaphysical consists in this, that God has granted more or less perfections to his creatures. It is plain that there is no disorder in this; it is even necessary as the source of order, for this very variety while harmoniously disposed constitutes the foundation of that beauty and order in the moral world which excites our admiration. It is the principle of society, the source of heroism and the origin of all the virtues.

2nd. Physical evil consists of the pains which afflict the human body in many ways. These are the consequences of the actual condition of man; and it derogates nothing from the perfections of God, that, though infinitely good, he has established this condition. For it may be demonstrated that the good is greater than the evil, even from this physical point of view, as is evident from the fact that there is no one who does not prefer to live rather than to die. Besides, these evils are the source of moral good to many, and thus become the occasion of eternal happiness: the greatest virtues have their origin in the existence of these evils or pains. Moreover, we know that physical pains are often the result of moral evil.

In a Christian sense the evil does not exist, but as punishment; original sin explains everything; but in this work we consider the question philosophically.

3d. Moral evil is sin. God was not obliged to prevent sin for these reasons:

(a) Not *on account of his sanctity or holiness*: God is holy if he be not sullied with sin and if he hate it; but such is the case.

(b) Not *on account of his justice:* God is just if he have established man in a condition good in itself, and if he do not punish him unjustly; but such is the case.

(c) Not *on account of his goodness:* God is good if he have granted to man liberty, which is good both in itself and in the intention of God; but such is the case.

(d) Not *on account of his wisdom:* God is wise if he have done nothing but for a good end, and have chosen the best means to reach that end; but such is the case. He proposed to reward the virtues of men, and gave them the most efficacious means that they might not abuse their liberty.

The objections to our arguments are taken from the fact of God's foreseeing the abuse which men would make of the liberty he gave them. The principles for refuting these objections are as follows: The intention of God was good, the gift was good, the foresight of God had no influence on human liberty, God helps human weakness, and, finally, all agree hat existence, as it is, is better than non-existence.

CHAPTER SECOND.

Of the Eternity of God.

Proposition.—*God is eternal.*

Argument: God is eternal if he be necessary, but God is necessary; then he is eternal.

Proof: We have already proved that God is necessary. A necessary being is one whose essence it is *to be;* and, since we cannot conceive a being without its essence, the necessary being must always have been: hence he is eternal.

If the necessary being were not eternal he would have been produced by another being, for he could not have produced himself, that is, he would be contingent; but we have proved that God is the necessary being, he is then eternal.

Several authors have considered the question whether there is succession in the eternity of God. We have seen that the necessary being is infinite, but infinity and succession in the same being involve a contradiction. Succession is composed of moments added to one another, each of course being limited; but the infinite excludes limitation, while succession includes series, a series being a collection of finite beings: hence, the infinite and series, or succession, are terms involving a contradiction. The eternity of God is therefore not successive, but simple, like his own being. God is. For him, there is neither past nor future, but all is present: his essence is *to be.*

CHAPTER THIRD.

Of the Immutability of God.

Proposition.—*God is immutable.*

Argument: God is immutable if immutability can be ascribed only to contingent beings, but such is the case, and hence God is immutable.

Proof: Mutation is the transition from one condition to another, consequently the transition from the possible to the real: hence mutation can be applied only to contingent beings, and the infinite and the mutable are terms involving a contradiction.

In God everything is infinite; hence nothing can be changed, either in his perfections or his decrees; there can be in him nothing which is contingent. God is then immutable.

In order to solve the objections which are advanced against this attribute of God, let it be remembered that in God there is neither past nor future. These words cannot be applied to God, to whom everything is present.

CHAPTER FOURTH.

Of the Liberty of God.

Liberty is the power of choosing. The object of liberty is either an act which brings to its author some perfection or imperfection, or else an act which brings to him neither perfection nor imperfection: hence we see that the object of liberty is within the limits of what is good.

Liberty may be considered as freedom either from

external force, otherwise called freedom from coaction; or as freedom from necessity, otherwise called freedom of election.

The acts may also be either exterior or interior. For God, the interior acts are those whose object is himself.

Evidently God is free from coaction; but, in his interior acts, he is not free from necessity.

The liberty of God has been attacked by the Pantheists, who, admitting only one substance, make every phenomenon a necessary modification of God; and also by the Optimists, but these deny God's liberty only indirectly.

We shall divide this chapter into three articles: in the first we shall demonstrate the fact of the liberty of God; in the second we shall explain and refute the doctrine of the Pantheists; and in the third that of the Optimists.

ARTICLE FIRST.—THE EXISTENCE OF THE LIBERTY OF GOD.

Proposition.—*God is free in his exterior acts.*

Argument: God is free if liberty is a perfection, and if no cause could have compelled him to create from necessity, but such is the case, and therefore he is free in his exterior acts.

Proof: Liberty is a perfection; for a being who is free, is independent in his acts and the supreme arbiter of what he does; and independence is better than dependence, and consequently an absolute perfection; but God being infinite possesses infinitely all absolute perfections; hence he is free.

God possesses infinitely all the perfections which are found in his creatures; but we are free, and therefore he must be free.

No cause could have obliged God to create from necessity: neither *his happiness* nor *his glory*, for in these he suffices for himself; nor *his internal perfections*, for if this were so we should conclude that God, considered in his essence, is not infinitely perfect, but certainly this would be untrue.

It appears difficult to reconcile the immutability of God with his liberty. Three systems have been formed for this purpose, but they are not satisfactory. It is enough for us that both attributes have been proved to exist in God: the difficulties spoken of only serve to show the weakness of human reason.

Article Second.—Pantheism.

Pantheism is the system of those who admit the existence of but one substance, which substance, according to them, is infinite. Hence, the Pantheists agree with the Atheists in making matter exist from necessity, and consequently in making it eternal and infinite.

The doctrines of Pantheism may be reduced to these three heads: First, what exists, exists from necessity; second, what exists forms one substance; and, third, this one substance is infinite.

The above principles are evidently false: For, in the first place, it has been proved that there is but one necessary being; and that we are contingent, since we have received our existence. Secondly, there is a multiplicity of substances in the world, if, for instance, there exists an essential difference between my soul and the bodies around me. Again, if there were but one substance, this substance would be either material or spiritual, or at the same time both spiritual and material; but certainly all the substances in the world are not spiritual only, or material only, nor are they at the same time both spiritual and material, for this would be a contradiction. Thirdly, as the infinite is simple, that is, not composed of parts, it is clear that matter cannot be infinite.

The doctrine of Pantheism is pernicious in its consequences, for these reasons: 1st. It takes away all obligation and sanction from the moral laws, since according to this system there is no superior being. We speak thus absolutely, although the Pantheist will say that conventions may be held and their decisions accepted for the sake of peace: we all know that no convention not approved of God can ever find the human conscience. 2nd. Pantheism destroys man's liberty, and consequently takes from him all responsibility for his actions; for if matter be necessary so also are its volitions or modifications, the actions of men, according to the Pantheists, being but modifications of the one necessary substance. 3d. Pantheism would oblige us to admit logically certain consequences which are evidently absurd; as, for instance, that God is a stone, a plant, or a beast.

Pantheism was taught among the ancients, in the Eleatic school; and, indirectly, by some writers of the middle ages. But the doctrine which we have explained is modern pantheism, as reduced to a system by Spinosa, a Jew, of Amsterdam, Holland.

Pantheism has been taught also in Germany, by Kant, Fichte, Hegel, &c. All those writers insist upon the unity of substance; there is according to them no distinction except a logical one, between the *ego* and the *non-ego* ("me" and "not me") that is, there is but a logical, and not a real, distinction between the subjective and the objective. This doctrine of Spinosa and the German philosophers is based upon the following definition of substance, which is ambiguous; "Substance is that which is in se (in itself), and which is conceived to exist by itself; that is, it is that of which we may conceive; without conceiving of some other being by which it might have been formed." Evidently there is here an allusion to the modification, which does not exist independently of the substance, and which presupposes substance in order that it should exist itself.

Pantheism is the doctrine of the French Communists, called Saint Simonists, Phalansteriens, Fourierists, &c.; and it is notorious what calamities have lately resulted from their doctrine in Europe, and especially in France.

Article Third.—Optimism.

Optimism is a system originated by Mallebranche and Leibnitz, in order to vindicate the providence of God and to refute the objections of Bayle and others against the goodness of God on account of the evil which exists in the world. Both Leibnitz and Mallebranche admit the existence of evil; but according to them the evil is necessary for the perfection of the universe, and does not detract from this perfection. According to Mallebranche, God was free to create, and could consequently have refrained from creating. He was also free to choose among several worlds equally perfect that which he wished to form; but, owing to the perfections of his attributes, he was not free to choose a less perfect world, rejecting others more perfect.

According to Leibnitz, God, on account of his wisdom and goodness, was not free not to create, nor was he free to create any but the most perfect world. God could not even choose among several worlds unequally perfect, taking one in preference to another. Still, even when God acts according to what is absolutely required by his attributes, he remains free.

Both systems must be rejected, first, because they destroy, at least indirectly, the liberty of God, notwithstanding the contrary assertion of both philosophers. They must also be rejected because they assume that the ultimate reason for the exterior acts of God is the goodness of the object of these acts; while, in fact, this ultimate reason for God's exterior acts is his own will, for which reason he may choose a less perfect object in preference to a more perfect one, if he wills it, provided this choice be not in derogation of any of his attributes.

Thirdly, their system must be rejected because its assertion that God was obliged to create the most perfect world involves an impossibility: for the most perfect world would be one of such perfection that none more perfect could be imagined; but the perfection of the world could never be such that a more perfect one might not be imagined; for however perfect it might become, it would still be finite, that is limited; and what is limited is capable of increase, that is, it is imperfect: hence, the most perfect world must be infinite in perfection, which is an impossibility. The systems of Mallebranche and Leibnitz must therefore be rejected.

CHAPTER FIFTH.

Of the Omnipotence and Independence of God.

1st. *Omnipotence* is the power of producing, or of bringing into existence, that which is merely possible. By what is possible, we mean that which does not exist, but the idea of which involves no contradiction.

Proposition.—*God is omnipotent*.

Argument: God is omnipotent if he can do whatever is possible; but such is the case, and hence he is omnipotent.

Proof: God can do whatever is possible: for either he has this infinite power, or else he can do nothing or only something; but the latter supposition cannot be correct, since, if it were so, God's power would not be so great as we may conceive it to be, and consequently not infinite. But he is infinite, and hence he can do everything which is possible; he is therefore omnipotent.

Note.—It is evident that God cannot do what is impossible; for instance, he could not make a square circle, because that involves a contradiction: the essence of a circle is roundness, and no being can have an essence other than its own; for, if it could, the being would both be and not be at the same time.

It is also plain that God cannot make what is infinite; for, if so, the infinite would have a beginning, that is a limitation, but the infinite has no limitation, no beginning, hence it cannot be produced by God.

2nd. Proposition.—*God is infinitely independent*.

Argument: God is infinitely independent if he depends on no one for his existence, or for the mode of that existence; but such is the case, and therefore he is infinitely independent.

Proof: Independence consists in this, that the being who is independent depends on no one for his existence, or for the mode of that existence. Such is the case in regard to God. We have demonstrated that he exists in himself (*a se*); hence he depends on no one for his existence. The second part is but a corollary of the first; for if God depends on no one for his existence he is equally independent as to the mode of that existence, since the mode, or modification, necessarily follows the substance.

CHAPTER SIXTH.

OF THE SIMPLICITY OF GOD.

This attribute of God has been denied by the Polytheists, the Pantheists, the Materialists and the Anthropomorphites. These last were heretics of the fourth century who, taking the words of Scripture in a literal sense, maintained that God has eyes, mouth, hands, &c.

Proposition.—*God is Simple.*

Argument: God is simple if he is infinite; but he is infinite, hence he is simple.

Proof: If God is not simple he is composed of parts; and these parts cannot be infinite, but must be finite. But God himself is infinite, and we cannot admit that a compound of finite parts, the essence of which is to be limited, can constitute a being which is infinite, or the essence of which is to be unlimited. Hence, God is simple; and hence, also, he is not corporeal. This latter conclusion is against the Anthropomorphites.

CHAPTER SEVENTH.

Of the Immensity of God.

We call that immense which cannot be measured. *The immensity of God* is that attribute by virtue of which his presence cannot be limited, or by virtue of which he is present to everything that exists: hence, immensity means the same as omnipresence; and, since God is an intelligence, he is omnipresent not only by his knowledge and operations, but also in his Substance.

Proposition.—*God is Immense.*

Argument: God is immense if he is infinite; but he is infinite, hence he is immense.

Proof: We have shown that God is infinite, that is, that he is without any limitation: hence, according to the definition, he is immense. He is therefore substantially present everywhere.

NOTE.—This substantial immensity of God is not of course a corporeal presence, but a spiritual one, since God is infinitely simple; for the same reason, although God is whole in each part of space, still his substance is not multiple. Finally, we may say correctly that God is everywhere and also that he is nowhere: in saying that he is nowhere, we mean that he does not occupy a limited point of space, or a space of certain distance or dimensions, as creatures do. Here again we meet with a difficulty in explaining how God can be simple and immense at the same time; but we have shown that he possesses both these attributes, and that they do not involve any contradiction.

CHAPTER EIGHTH.

OF THE KNOWLEDGE OF GOD.

Men before knowing must conceive, judge and reason; but such is not the case in regard to the knowledge of God. He knows, or rather sees, everything. All philosophers admit, first, that God alone knows *himself* perfectly; second, that everything past is present to him, for otherwise his immutability would be destroyed; third, that everything present, even the most secret things are known to him; fourth, that he knows everything which is possible and that he realizes those same things; and, fifth, that he knows all future things which are necessary, that is, which flow necessarily from the laws established by him.

In regard to those future things which are called contingent, that is, those things which may happen, but which are dependent on the free choice of men, Cicero and many other pagan writers, and afterwards the Socinians, as well as certain modern theorists, have maintained that God has only a contingent knowledge.

But it is certain that God knows all future things, even those which are conditional and contingent; and this may be proved in the following manner:

1st. God is immutable; hence he knows everything, for otherwise he might acquire knowledge, and consequently change.

2nd. God is infinite. But if God did not know everything we might conceive a being more perfect than God, and this would destroy his infinity.

3d. God is eternal. Eternity is the permanence of existence, or being. Eternity is one and simple, and we have proved that it cannot be successive; consequently, such words as "prevision," "prescience," and "conjecture," are inaccurate when applied to the eternal being, that is, to God. God is, and, consequently, knows; and neither in his being nor in his knowing can there be any limitation, any priority or posteriority.

4th. All mankind have ever been convinced of this truth.

The scholastics have asked in what way it is that God sees all things, and what is the character of his knowledge. All admit that it is more perfect to know a thing directly than indirectly, or to see a thing in itself, that is, in its essence, rather than in a being distinct from the thing. Hence it follows that God sees himself, and all possible things, as well as all future necessary things, in their own essence.

St. Thomas says that God also sees future free and contingent things in their essence, that is, that he sees them in his eternal and immutable decrees; for nothing, even a free action, happens except by a decree of God, in such a way that in our free actions God is an efficient cause. But Molina and his disciples contend that with such a system it is impossible to defend human liberty; and they say that God sees the future as contingent on the free determinations of his creatures. We can accept either system.

In order to answer objections to the foreknowledge of God, we have but to remember the words of St. Jerome: "The actions of men foreseen by God do not happen because God foresees them, but God foresees them because they are going to happen."

CHAPTER NINTH.

OF THE WISDOM OF GOD.

Wisdom is that attribute according to which a being proposes to himself a good end and takes the most proper means to reach that end; but God has this attribute, for, first, he is infinitely perfect, second, the order existing in the world proclaims his wisdom, and, third, we have shown that God possesses in an eminent degree all the perfections found in his creatures.

CHAPTER TENTH.

Of the Sanctity and Veracity of God.

Sanctity consists in the love of what is good and the hatred of what is evil: it is evident that such an attribute must be found in a being who is infinitely perfect.

Veracity consists in this, that a being can neither deceive nor be deceived: God being holy cannot deceive, and having a knowledge which is infinite, he cannot be deceived.

CHAPTER ELEVENTH.

Of the Goodness and Happiness of God.

Goodness, or benignity, is that attribute by which a being is inclined to do good to others gratuitously. Evidently such an attribute is a perfection, and consequently it is an attribute of God. This all men in all ages have believed: God has always been called *Deus optimus maximus.* "God very good and very great." To the goodness of God we must refer his mercy, which is rather an attribute in a theological sense, but which is also infinite.

Happiness consists in the enjoyment of the good and the absence of the evil: but God being independent cannot be subject to evil, and being infinitely perfect he must possess and of course enjoy all good. Hence God is infinitely good and infinitely happy.

CHAPTER TWELFTH.

OF THE JUSTICE OF GOD.

Justice is the attribute according to which we give to others what belongs to them. God of course possesses this attribute, for if he did not act thus, he would not be equitable, and consequently not infinitely perfect. We might here, if necessary, cite the testimony of men; but all agree on this point.

CHAPTER THIRTEENTH.

OF THE PROVIDENCE OF GOD.

We divide this last Chapter on the Attributes of God into two Articles.

ARTICLE FIRST.—THE EXISTENCE OF PROVIDENCE.

Providence is the care which God extends over his creatures; or, it is the action by which he directs his creatures, either the reasonable or the unreasonable, to the end which is proper, to each individually, and to all in general.

The Epicureans, the Stoics, who held the doctrine of fatalism, and some modern philosophers contending, that God's providence would destroy man's liberty, and that God is too great and too high to take such care of us, deny the existence of providence. Against them we establish this

Proposition.—*God's providence exists and extends to all things.*

Argument: The existence of providence must be accepted if it be required by those attributes of God which are believed by all, and which are necessary in order to explain the order of the world; but such is the case, and hence providence does exist, and must extend to all things.

Proof: 1st. All admit that it is good, that it is a perfection, to take care of what we have produced; hence, God, who is infinitely perfect, must have this perfection.

Providence is required by the wisdom and goodness of God. God's wisdom requires that he should do what is necessary in order that his creatures may reach the end he has designed for them; and we are so ignorant, so weak, and so wickedly disposed, that without providence we could not reach this end.

The goodness of God requires that he should do what is necessary in order that we may obtain happiness; but we have just seen that without God's providence we could not reach our end, hence we could not be happy, and God would not be good: but since God is good providence must exist.

2nd. All people, in all ages, and in all countries, have believed in the existence of providence, as might easily be shown by the testimony of Christian and pagan writers; and this testimony, so universal, so uniform, so constant, and concerning such an important question, is a criterion of certitude: we may therefore again conclude that providence exists.

3d. The constancy and uniformity of the effects, or rather of the order perpetuated in the world, is after all the most striking proof of the care which God takes of his creatures: and if this argument is so clear, and so generally confessed by every one, in regard to the physical world, *a fortiori* it is likewise conclusive in regard to the moral world.

To these proofs we may add the following consideration: Existence is something contingent to us, since it does not belong to our essence; consequently, existence must be renewed at every instant of our life. Then, in order that we may live, it is necessary that God perpetuate, that is, renew at every instant, the act of his will by which he created us. Providence is therefore a continued creation; and, so far as God's will is concerned, it is a necessity. But with God, to will and to act are the same; hence the action of God upon us during our life is constant, and this is what we mean by his providence.

In order to answer the objections to this proposition, we have but to observe that the preservation of his creatures does not injure the majesty of God any more than their creation; and that such care cannot cause trouble or grief to God who is infinitely happy and immutable.

ARTICLE SECOND.—CONSEQUENCES OF THE EXISTENCE OF PROVIDENCE IN REGARD TO THE FREE ACTIONS OF MEN.

From the definition given above, it follows that God directs everything in the world towards its own end; and, consequently, that this action must have some influence over the free actions of men. This influence may be natural or supernatural. It is natural when the actions are considered without reference to future life, and supernatural when these actions are considered with reference to future life.

This supernatural influence is God's *grace*, a subject belonging to theology.

We have here to examine only the natural influence of God over the free actions of man. We shall first consider whether this influence exists, and if so what is its nature.

I. Does this influence of God exist?

The existence of this influence has been denied by several modern philosophers. But that the influence does exist is certain, for (a) God is the primary cause, and this attribute requires that everything which is a perfection in the creature should proceed from God; but evidently the good use of liberty is a perfection, nay, even the greatest perfection in man, hence this good use proceeds from God. Good use here signifies the free and right determination of men, but under the influence of God, since this way of acting, which is a perfection, must proceed from him.

(b) We may here again bring forward the consent of mankind. We all pray to God, that he may guide us, correct us, help us, inspire us, &c.

Evidently, this influence takes place only for the good use of liberty. In regard to its wrong use, God cannot have an immediate, but only a mediate influence on man's actions, in the sense that he has granted liberty, of which a bad use is made against his suggestions: his sanctity forbids that he should act immediately in that case.

II. What is the nature of this influence?

The Molinists pretend that this influence is positive and direct, but not on our will, which it neither moves nor determines, but simply helps, and with which it acts in concurrence for the performance of actions, so long as our will remains within the limits of what is good. As this assistance consists in affording a concourse of circumstances the most suitable for the determination, the followers of this system have been called Congruists.

The Thomists maintain that the above system too much restrains the actions of God, who is the primary cause of everything which is a perfection in his creatures; and they contend that the influence of providence is direct even upon the will, but however that God, whose knowledge is infinite, keeps human liberty always safe.

It seems difficult to conceive how man's liberty is preserved, according to the system of the Thomists; and equally difficult to understand how the supreme dominion of God is respected, according to the system of the Molinists.

This question, like many others, occasioned by the difficulty of explaining the attributes of God, became the subject matter of many books, which now, as Bouvier says, sleep in the dust, and the question is not solved, and remains insoluble.

There are other opinions, and especially that of St. Augustine, but they are rather theological than philosophical, and consequently we shall omit them, and here finish this treatise on Theodicy, which is the first part of Pneumatology, or spiritual metaphysics.

THIRD DISSERTATION.

ON PSYCHOLOGY.

The word Psychology is derived from the Greek ψυχη λογος, and signifies a discourse upon the soul. We may define this branch of pneumatology to be the science which has for its object the general knowledge of the human soul.

Psychology is divided into two parts: the first treating of the human soul more according to experience than reason; and the second treating of it more according to reason than experience. The first is called experimental psychology, and the second rational psychology. We shall treat of these two parts in succession.

PART FIRST.—EXPERIMENTAL PSYCHOLOGY.

Experimental Psychology may be defined to be the science which treats of the faculties of the human soul by the method of experience. According to this definition we shall naturally divide the subject of experimental psychology into as many parts as there are faculties of the human soul.

We find in the soul three faculties, or general attributes: namely, activity, which is the fundamental attribute, and the sensibility and the intellect, which are the faculties that excite the soul to action.

Since activity is not put in motion in the soul until it is first excited by the sensibility and the intellect, we shall treat first of the sensibility, next of the intellect and afterwards of activity.

CHAPTER FIRST.

Of Sensibility.

The Sensibility of the soul may be considered either in general or particular.

Sensibility, in general, is the faculty by which the human soul experiences emotions which are ordinarily pleasant or unpleasant. A pleasant emotion is called *pleasure*, and an unpleasant one *pain*.

The elements of sensibility are two. As soon as the soul perceives a sensation it instinctively turns to the object causing the sensation; we have therefore two elements, the sensation perceived and the reactive motion of the soul: in the first case the soul is passive, and in the second it is active, but this activity is instinctive and necessary.

This sensible emotion is merely passive and subjective, and is thus distinguished from the intellectual perception, which is a modification of the soul merely passive, but also objective; because the intellectual perception represents an object as distinct from the modification itself.

The reactive motion of the soul is called by the moralists *motus primo primus*, and its ordinary appellation is *appetite*. This reaction is *attractive* when the emotion is agreeable, and repulsive when it is disagreeable.

The source from which these attractive and repulsive emotions, or all the appetites of our soul, proceed, is the love of ourselves.

Sensibility, in particular, is exterior and physical when the emotion is produced by the action of the organs of sense, and interior when this emotion is produced without such action.

(A) *Physical sensibility* is the power of experiencing sensation. By *sensation* we understand the emotion which the soul experiences on account of some action of the organs of sense. Three elements, then, are found in physical sensibility: the organic impression which precedes and causes the sensation; the sensation itself; and the appetite, or the reaction after the sensation.

(a) The organic impression is the impression made on one of the organs of sense by an external body, and transmitted to the brain by the nerves.

The senses are five in number: taste, touch, smell, hearing and sight. No sensation is experienced before the impression made on the organ of sense has reached the brain. The brain is an organ consisting of a soft, whitish, nerve-like substance, situated in the skull. That part in the upper front part of the head is the direct and immediate organ, not only of physical sensibility, but also of interior sensibility, of the intellect, and even of the will; so that if that part of the brain is removed or paralyzed the man loses his power of feeling, of understanding, and even of controlling the acts of his will.

The brain is divided into two parts, or lobes, one on the right side and the other on the left, and each part is subdivided into many smaller ones. Upon these divisions the system of the phrenologists is built.

The nerves are either sensitive or motive. The sensitive nerves are those that transmit the impressions made on the organs of sense to the brain; and the motive nerves, or motors, are those that serve, as we might say, as the tools of the will. How these impressions are conveyed to the brain, and how the desires of the will are carried back again, are questions to which no answer has been given.

(b) *Sensation.*—From what has been said it is easy to see the difference between sensation and the organic impression, which causes sensation. Sensations are either pleasant or unpleasant; and our power of knowing by means of the nerves the place of the impression enables us to determine what part of the body feels pleasure or pain.

There are some sensations which we may call indifferent. Although in morals no human act is indifferent in regard to salvation, yet we may accept the opinion of a large number of authors who consider many of our sensations as indifferent, that is, as affording neither pain nor pleasure, or, at most, very little of either pleasure or pain.

(c) *Appetite.*—Appetite is the reactive motion of the soul after it has experienced a sensation, whether agreeable or disagreeable. It is now customary to call the appetite resulting from an unpleasant or repulsive sensation a *repugnance*. We can now readily understand the difference between sensation and appetite.

It is not by sensation only that appetite is excited in the soul: the remembrance of a sensation is sufficient to produce appetite.

Appetites are *periodic*, as that of hunger, &c.; and *accidental*, as that for a certain kind of food, &c.

It is obvious that the end to be obtained by appetite is the preservation of the body.

(B) *Interior sensibility* is the power of experiencing sentiments. A *sentiment* is the emotion produced in the soul by an intellectual notion. A sentiment differs from a sensation in two respects: first, a sentiment is produced by an intellectual notion, while a sensation is produced by an impression on the organ of one of the senses; and, second, the nature of the resulting emotions of pleasure or pain are different.

The reactive emotion arising from a sentiment is called *passion*.

Interior sensibility considered in relation to its object is three-fold in character: 1st, in relation to the personal affections, 2nd, in relation to social desires, and 3d, in relation to those sentiments which involve a certain conception of pure reason.

(a) Personal affections. These are the dispositions, good or bad, with which we regard our fellow men; and which determine us to wish them good or evil; they are accordingly either benevolent or malevolent.

The benevolent affections are either particular or general, and the others universal. The particular benevolent affections are those of the family, friendship, gratitude, commiseration, &c. The general benevolent affections are charity, love of country, &c. Among the malevolent affections we may mention rivalry, envy, &c.

The principal distinctions between the benevolent and the malevolent affections are: first, a benevolent affection is always accompanied with an agreeable emotion; second, a benevolent disposition is natural to man; and, third, in regard to the object, benevolence is more extensive than malevolence.

(b) Social desires. These are emotions of the soul by which we are inclined to seek for certain advantages that are found only in society, as reputation, power, &c. These desires may be reduced to five: 1st, the desire for social companionship, which is natural to all men; 2nd, the desire of knowing; 3d, the desire of acquiring esteem and consideration; 4th, the desire of superiority, and 5th, the desire of property. These words need no explanation.

(c) Sentiments involving some conception of pure reason. There exist within us certain sentiments which originate in the soul by the influence of the conceptions of pure reason; as, for example, by the conceptions of the ideas of *truth*, of *beauty*, of the *infinite*, &c.

The chief sentiments of this kind are: the sentiment of truth; the sentiment of beauty, or the æsthetic sentiment; the sentiment of goodness, or the moral sentiment; the religious sentiment; and the sentiment of the infinite. There is such an affinity between the objects of these sentiments and our intelligence that the soul cannot perceive them without experiencing some agreeable emotion, and this emotion is called the love of truth, of beauty, of goodness, &c.

CHAPTER SECOND.
Of the Intellect.

We have already, in Logic and in the Introduction, examined most of the notions concerning the intellect, and we shall now only briefly recapitulate them.

The intellect is the thinking power. The faculties of the intellect may be divided into two classes, the perceptive faculties by which the mind perceives, and the reflexive faculties, by which the mind makes use of these perceptions. This Chapter is therefore divided into two Articles, to which we shall add a third on the nature and origin of ideas.

Article First.—The Perceptive Faculties.

There are two kinds of perception, the perception of contingent things, otherwise called experimental perception or experience; and the perception of necessary things, otherwise called rational perception or pure reason, or simply reason.

(A) The experimental perceptive faculties are: Consciousness; memory, to which may be added what is called the association of ideas; and the perception of the senses.

It is well to observe here that there is an essential difference between sensation and the perception of the senses. As we have said, sensation is a phenomenon purely subjective. For instance, the sensation of smell is altogether an affection of the soul, and represents nothing distinct from this sensation; for if there were a representation of something accompanying the sensation it would not belong to the sensation itself, but to the perception or the imagination. The perception of the senses, on the contrary, is a phenomenon both subjective and objective, which represents something which is outside the soul. The confusion of these two notions was the origin of sensism.

The errors generally attributed to the perception of the senses come from three sources: 1st, dreams and delirium, 2nd, affirmation of more than the senses perceive, and 3d, weakness or unsound condition of some of the organs of sense. To avoid mistakes from these sources, we should affirm nothing more than we really perceive, and if possible use more than one sense to observe the same phenomenon. Besides, we should renew our observations under different circumstances.

(B) The rational perceptions are, first, ideas, or rational conceptions, the principal of which are those of being (*idea entis*), of unity, of infinity, of substance, of cause, of truth, of beauty, and of goodness, concerning all of which we have already spoken sufficiently; and, second, the necessary truths, or the principles of pure reason, which we have explained in the Dissertation on the motives of certitude.

Article Second.—The Reflexive Faculties.

The reflexive faculties are those by which the soul exercises its activity upon the perceptions. They are, as we have explained in Part First: Attention, abstraction, judgment, reasoning, imagination, and the expression and transmission of thought by language.

The imagination is that faculty by which the soul represents to itself an object under a sensible form, without the present or actual exercise of the perception of the senses. The imagination may be creative, as well as reproductive; for we may by imagination represent to ourselves certain intellectual notions under sensible forms.

The imagination is affected by the vicissitudes of the body and the influence of physical agents more than any other intellectual faculty: it is modified by the influence of age, temperament, sickness, manner of living and diversity of climate.

When the imagination is well directed it affords much aid towards the happiness and moral improvement of mankind; but when badly directed, especially when sustained by the reading of novels and bad books, its influence is most pernicious.

The expression and transmission of our ideas by language is a subject which must be treated more fully.

(a) *General Notions.*

Language, in general, is any sensible sign by which men may communicate to one another their thoughts, feelings and affections: it is either natural or acquired.

Natural language is that which men use and understand without any previous instruction; such as gestures, looks, shouts, &c. This kind of language, which is also called gesticulation, is very expressive in certain circumstances, but generally is too vague, uncertain and incomplete.

Acquired language is that which can neither be expressed nor understood without previous instruction and knowledge of the native tongue. This kind of language is either spoken or written. Spoken language, being uttered by the tongue and other organs of speech, is language properly so called, or the *tongue*, as we say the English tongue, the French tongue, &c.

Language is natural to men, in the sense that they have suitable organs for its use; but it is also conventional, in the sense that the meaning given to the sounds issuing from the organs of speech is fixed almost altogether by the agreement of men.

It is clear that spoken language is far more useful than that which we have called natural language, or gesture.

Written language is a collection of fixed and permanent figures, by the use of which men give expression to their ideas. It is of three kinds, ideographic, or picture writing (as the figures in arithmetic, algebra, geometry and chemistry); alphabetic; and hieroglyphic, which is a mixture of the other two.

(b) *Language Considered in Relation to Thought.*

Language is not the producing cause of our ideas, but it is necessary in order that the human intellect should attain the degree of perfection of which it is capable. In regard to abstract and purely intellectual ideas, language is necessary to develop and preserve them; for it is impossible without language to meditate upon things which do not belong to the sensible order, as, for instance, God and his attributes, &c.

In order that the language be well composed, it is necessary that it be full, clear and harmonious. The rules to be followed in its use are given in the text-books on grammar.

(c) *The Origin of Language.*

The enquiry on this subject is two-fold: we have first to consider the question of fact, and secondly that of possibility.

FIRST.—THE QUESTION OF FACT.

I. It is certain from Genesis that God gave to our first parents a supernatural knowledge of articulate or spoken language.

II. The most ancient traditions of all nations agree in admitting the existence of what they call the golden age, during which God conversed with men and instructed them.

III. All history is silent concerning an invention of language.

IV. The study of philosophy has shown conclusively that all languages have had a common origin, or that there was a primitive language which furnished the roots of all other tongues; and it is surely more simple and reasonable to explain this fact by the supernatural gift of language to man in the beginning, than by the invention of a first language which must have been imperfect and incomplete, and which consequently could not have been the original of all languages.

SECOND.—THE QUESTION OF POSSIBILITY.

Is it possible that our first parents could of themselves have invented language?

I. All the materialists and sensists affirm that our first parents could have done this. Some Christian philosophers hold the same opinion, and say: First, that men can naturally express what they feel by some external signs, and consequently that, if they can think before speaking, they can manifest their thoughts by spoken language; but, they farther assert, men can think before speaking, and hence could have invented language. Secondly, they say, that by attention men can have ideas of individual things, and afterwards express these ideas in words; then pass from this point to abstraction, generalization, &c., and so gradually form language.

II. De Bonald is the principal defender of the opinion that it is impossible that men should have invented language; and most of the Catholic philosophers side with him. They say, first, that without language it is imposible to acquire reflexive ideas of immaterial things; and this is proved by daily experience and by the mental state of the deaf and dumb who have not been taught an artificial language, as well as by the state of mind of certain unfortunate persons who have lived in the wilderness without human society from their infancy.

Secondly, as is shown in the case of children, abstract and general ideas, even of material things, cannot be acquired, except gradually and with the knowledge of the language: these ideas require reflexion, and reflexion requires words. Thirdly, in order to invent language it would first be necessary to know its law and structure; but these cannot be known without reflexion, and the same difficulty occurs as before. Fourthly, language could not be invented by one man, since he could not be understood by the rest of men, nor could he obtain their consent to use the language formed by him; nor could it be invented by a number of men, for this would suppose an agreement, and no agreement is possible without language. Fifthly, they conclude language cannot have been invented gradually, since it forms a whole of which all the parts exist at the same time.

Neither of these opinions is sufficiently conclusive. Either, however, may be accepted without opposing the Catholic doctrine.

ARTICLE THIRD.—THE NATURE AND ORIGIN OF OUR IDEAS.

1st. The Nature of our Ideas.

We have already spoken of this subject in *Logic;* but there we considered ideas especially in regard to the objects which they represent. We have now to examine the question subjectively, and enquire whether our ideas of things, corporeal or incorporeal, are only modifications of the mind representing objects to itself; or whether they are images distinct from these modifications and also from the objects represented. According to the first hypothesis, there are but two things to be considered in connection with the idea, namely, the subject and the object, while, according to the second hypothesis, there is, besides the subject and the object, an image which is a medium between the two. Philosophers are divided in opinion on this question. Arnauld, Thomas Reed and Scotists advocate the first hypothesis; while Aristotle, Democritus, Mallebranche, Locke and the Materialists defend the second. Some of these latter consider the medium to be a material image, which is absurd.

It seems probable that the first hypothesis is the correct one; for the other is entirely gratuitous, and besides does not solve the difficulty, which is: How does the soul, a spiritual substance, see corporeal things? This difficulty reappears on the introduction of the medium.

2d. *The Origin of our Ideas.*

Ideas are pure, or rational, when their objects are necessary things, and empiric when they represent contingent things. But as empiric ideas come from experience, we need not here enquire of the origin of this sort of ideas, but only of those which are pure, or rational; besides, ideas ought not to be considered as abstract, but as concrete, for undoubtedly abstract ideas come from abstraction.

The question then is: What is the origin, or the source of concrete rational ideas, such as the idea of existence, of unity, of truth, of substance, &c.

There have been three opinions entertained by philosophers concerning the origin of ideas: that of the Sensists, that of those who teach the doctrine of innate ideas and that concerning the intuition of God, *entis simpliciter.*

(a) *The System of the Sensists.*

This is the system of those who derive all our ideas, even rational ideas, from the senses. Their axiom is: There is nothing in the intellect which was not first in the senses. All the Sensists agree that at the time of its creation the soul is like a sheet of blank paper, void of all ideas.

There is a difference between the Materialists and the Sensists; the former contend that the soul is a material substance, the latter do not. Among the Sensists we find the names of Bacon, Locke, Condillac, Laromiguiere.

This system ought to be rejected, if it is true that rational ideas cannot come from the senses; but it is true that these ideas cannot come from this source, either directly by the perception of the senses or indirectly by reflexion: for the senses perceive only bodies and their phenomena; and reflexion, acting upon ideas of contingent things, can derive nothing from them but what they contain, that is, what is contingent and mutable. Consequently, reflexion cannot derive from ideas of contingent things the ideas of truth, infinity, justice, &c., the objects of which are necessary and immutable things. This conclusion is strictly logical, and established upon the principle of contradiction.

(b) *The Doctrine of Innate Ideas.*

This is the doctrine of those who say that the mind is possessed of ideas which it did not acquire by its own power, but which were given to it by God, probably at the moment of its creation. Those who hold this doctrine say also that these ideas are not *actually* present to the mind at the moment of its creation, but only *habitually* present, and, as it were, remain slumbering in the soul, even as certain notions are stored up in the memory without being actually thought of until they are called forth by an effort of the mind. In like manner, they say, when reason becomes active these ideas become actual, or actively present, and the attention of the soul is directed towards them.

The defenders of the doctrine of innate ideas claim that Descartes and Leibnitz favor their system. Descartes says that "some ideas are born with us, and that the germs of truth are deposited in our souls and gradually come to light by the activity of reason." Leibnitz speaks in the same sense, and compares these germs to the veins in marble which form the figure of some object: the object needs only the hand of the artist to bring it forth.

It is evident that we cannot pronounce this system altogether false. The objections to it are: First, that if these ideas were in the mind we should have some consciousness of their presence; but no one can say positively that we have this consciousness. Second, this doctrine explains nothing if it is meant by it that we have in the mind certain dispositions only, or mere faculties, according to the explanation of Descartes and Leibnitz; if, however, it is meant by the doctrine, that at the moment of creation there are in the soul *virtual* notions, the supposition is gratuitous. Accordingly we may make another supposition, which is that, instead of those ideas, which are improperly called innate, the soul receives notions, at every moment, by the intuition of God; and this is the third system.

(c) *The Doctrine of the Intuition of God.*

This is the doctrine of those who maintain that rational ideas come into the mind by the intuitive perception of the simple being, or of God. According to this doctrine, which is the true one, God is present to our intellect and is seen by it; and from this perception the idea of the simple being, that is the idea of God, is present to our mind: and as the simple being is also infinite, necessary, eternal, &c., the intuition of this being contains in itself and produces in our mind the ideas of infinity, necessity, eternity, &c., in a word, all the rational ideas, which, after all, are nothing else than the idea of the simple being considered in itself.

This doctrine has been held by St. Augustine, St. Anselm, St. Bonaventure, Bossuet and many others.

We must observe that this intuition is not the beatific vision, which we can enjoy only in heaven; but is an intuition by which we may see God obscurely, and as it were, to use the Apostle's expression, in an enigma.

This doctrine satisfactorily explains the origin of ideas; still it is only a hypothesis.

CHAPTER THIRD.
Of Activity.

Activity is the power or faculty of acting: it is both interior and exterior. Interior activity is the soul's activity, considered independently of its action on the body; while exterior activity, on the contrary, is the soul's activity, considered with reference to the movements of the body: exterior activity has therefore been called the motrix faculty.

Interior activity is twofold, free and spontaneous; the latter must not be confounded with the soul's passivity.

Spontaneous activity is exercised in two ways, from instinct and from habit. Instinct differs from habit in this, that instinct proceeds from nature while habit is the result of a frequent repetition of the same acts. Instinct is found in animals as well as in men, and in children as well as in adults. Habit has been defined as the disposition to act acquired from a frequent repetition of the same acts. The soul and the body have each their own habits. It is evident that actions proceeding from mere habit are not free in themselves, though they may be so indirectly, that is, in their cause.

Free activity, or the liberty of the soul, will now be treated at large, forming the chief part of this chapter. The other subjects belong directly to theology.

The Freedom of the Human Soul.

We first give a definition of the will: The *will* is that faculty by which the soul chooses the good proposed to it by the intellect and avoids evil. Hence we conclude that nothing is willed unless it first be known.

The will is either necessary or free. In the first case, the one who wills cannot refrain from willing, and this is will properly so called; in the second case, one may refrain from willing that which is proposed by the intellect and choose something else, and this is called freedom. Freedom, therefore, is the power either to will or to refrain from willing; or, more simply, it is the power of choosing.

Among the philosophers who have denied the freedom of the will, we find, first, the Stoics, who were strict fatalists; second, the Pantheists, who cannot admit freedom without being in contradiction with themselves; third, the Manicheans, who pretended that we do good or evil according as the good or the evil principle inspires us; fourth, the Mahometans, who are fatalists; fifth, several modern religious systems which teach that we are predestined to do good by grace, and to do evil by concupiscence, thus confounding the notions of the voluntary and the free, and of course destroying freedom; sixth, the followers of Cousin and Gall, who indirectly teach fatalism; and, seventh, the Materialists, whose system, like that of the Pantheists, destroys human liberty.

NOTE.—Euler and some other philosophers have

METAPHYSICS. 159

contended that freedom is essential to spiritual substances. We feel constrained to deny this, and to say that God might have created us without liberty, at least without the liberty of doing wrong.

We have now to discuss the question as to whether we have the liberty of choosing, and will proceed to prove the

Proposition.—*The human mind is truly free.*

Argument: That ought to be admitted as true which is proved to be true by the testimony of consciousness, by the consent of mankind, by the absurd consequences of fatalism and by reason; but such is the case with the above proposition, and hence the human soul is free.

Proof: First. Consciousness. We have seen that consciousness is an infallible motive of judging of the present state of the soul. Now, we feel sure that in many of our actions we are free: we perceive that there is an essential difference between the actions which are performed with deliberation and those which are done without deliberation. The remorse that follows our bad actions helps us to make this distinction more evident. We may therefore conclude that the freedom of the will is proved by our own consciousness.

Second. The consent of mankind is a clear and powerful proof in this case. We find everywhere, and in all ages, laws, treaties, rewards, punishments, &c. Among themselves men naturally use entreaties, threats, exhortations, &c. Even the fatalists do not deny these facts, although they pretend to believe that this general persuasion proceeds from necessity. But we cannot admit that God, in his wisdom and love of truth, would permit all men to remain in such a state of delusion; and we therefore hold this consent of mankind as conclusive in favor of the freedom of the human soul.

Third. If the doctrine of fatalism were admitted, we should be but machines, deprived of reason. It would be absurd to speak of reasoning, deliberation, prudence, wisdom, &c., or of a distinction between virtue and vice or good and evil. There would be no merit in being a poet, an orator, or a philosopher, since necessity would compel certain persons to fill these positions. No one is willing to admit the existence of these consequences, which, however, are logically true if we are not free.

Fourth. Reason. We might here use an *argumentum ad hominem*. Would those philosophers who deny the existence of human liberty refrain from asking for punishment for any one who should strike or rob them? And yet, if they were logical, they would not consider those persons guilty who do these things. The illogical conduct of the fatalists themselves then shows that we are free.

We conclude:

1st. That the existence of our freedom is as clear as that of our thought.

2nd. That the denial of our freedom leads to the denial of certitude itself.

3d. That the existence of human freedom must be considered a primary truth.

It is in the doctrine of the moderate fatalists that we find objections raised against the existence of human freedom. By moderate fatalists we mean those philosophers who considering the strength of our physical nature, blinded more or less as it is by ignorance, habit or prejudice, exaggerate its influence over the determination of the will.

That this influence exists, and is in some cases very strong and very pressing, is of course true; but it can never have such power over our determination as to make us act from necessity. We may always ascertain that we have been free, even in those actions in which our temper, our habits, &c., have had most influence over us.

PART SECOND.—RATIONAL PSYCHOLOGY.

CHAPTER FIRST.

Of the Nature of the Human Soul, or of its Spirituality.

Those philosophers who admit the spirituality of the human soul are called Spiritualists, and those who deny it are called Materialists. Besides the school of Epicurus, we may rank among the Materialists, Locke, La Mettrie, Voltaire, Cabanis, Helvetius, d'Holbach and Diderot.

Among the ancients many admitted the spirituality of the soul, as Cicero and Aristotle.

Proposition.—*The soul is a simple substance, and absolutely distinct from matter.*

Argument: Two substances cannot be identical when they have opposite properties; but such is the case in regard to the soul and matter,

Proof: In order to prove the above proposition we will establish the fact that the soul is endowed with three properties which matter cannot have: the power of thinking, that of judging, and a free will, or activity.

I. *The soul has the power of thinking*, a power which cannot be found in any material substance, that is, in a substance which has extension and is capable of division; for if a material substance could have the power of thought, (1) the whole thought must be located in the whole substance, or (2) in each part of the substance, or (3) in one part only.

The first hypothesis cannot be accepted; for if it were true we should have to admit that thought may be divided into as many parts as there are in the substance, and consequently there would be no part which would be conscious of the whole thought or perceive its entire object.

The second hypothesis is equally absurd; for if it were true, the thought would be multiple, instead of divisible, but we feel that our thought is one.

The third hypothesis is also inadmissible, because the same difficulties come back. This part of the matter would itself be matter, and consequently divisible, and of course the thought must again be either divisible or multiple, and this is against the general conviction and feeling of our consciousness that the power of thinking is simple.

II. *The soul has the power of judging.* In order to compare there must be a comparer who examines the two notions to be compared; this comparer therefore must have the attribute of unity, but unity cannot be found where there is divisibility, that is, in matter. Hence this power belongs to a simple substance.

III. *The human soul is active.* We have proved that we are free; to be free is, first, to be active; but matter has no activity, being inert by nature: hence the soul must be an immaterial substance.

We might add other observations to the above: First, that taken from the identity of the thinking principle within us. We are conscious of this identity. We feel that we are now the same beings that we have ever been; and yet our bodies have been changed many times, being constantly renewed.

Second, that taken from the consciousness which we have at the same time of several sensations of a different character: I see, hear, smell, taste and touch at the same time, and am conscious that it is the same principle that perceives these various sensations. If, according to Epicurus, this principle were nothing else than the organs of the different senses, I could be conscious of but one sensation at the same time.

Third, that drawn from the consent of mankind may be added to the above, and we conclude that the immateriality of the soul is proved.

In order to answer the objections made against this proposition, let us observe that from the mutual influence of the soul and body over each other we cannot conclude that the two substances are identical, for these reasons:

(a) There is no contradiction in the action of a spiritual substance on a material one. (b) As God, who is a spiritual substance, acts upon material creatures, so may the soul act upon the body. (c) Many examples show these substances to be different; as very often a powerful mind is found in a weak and feeble body. (d) The body is to the soul what a musical instrument is to a musician: the musician tunes his instrument by degrees, and so the soul acts on the body during all the periods of our existence.

From what has been said we may conclude, first, that the soul is a substance endowed with activity, sensibility, intellect and freedom; and, second, that it is a substance which is a unit in every man, simple and always identical with itself.

CHAPTER SECOND.

Of the Union of the Soul with the Body.

From the last chapter it follows that the human soul and the human body are of different natures; but between them there is the closest union, the effects of which we experience at every instant. All admit this union, but in regard to the manner of explaining it several systems have been invented.

First system. This is called the system of physical influence, according to which the soul has a real influence over the body, as well as the body over the soul. This influence is called physical, not that it is material, but because the soul acts on the body as really and directly as one physical object would act upon another. This system was the only one received before the time of Mallebranche and Leibnitz, and even now it is generally accepted.

METAPHYSICS. 165

The second system, that of a plastic or operating mediator, is taught by those who believe that there is between the soul and the body a middle substance, by the aid of which the soul and the body mutually act upon each other. According to the philosophers who teach this doctrine, this mediator is an active and incorporeal substance, but is deprived of sensibility and intelligence.

The third system, that of occasional causes, is the one taught by Mallebranche. According to this system there is no real action of the soul upon the body, or of the body upon the soul: but the operations of the mind are only occasions, and these being present God himself acts upon the body; in like manner, the modifications of the body are occasions, which being also present, God modifies the mind, that is, excites sensations in it.

The fourth system, that of a pre-established harmony, is the system of Leibnitz. This philosopher teaches that there is no direct action of the soul upon the body, or of the body upon the soul; nor does God act directly upon the body on account of the operations of the mind, nor upon the mind on account of the modifications of the body; but He so disposes, or prepares, both body and soul at the time of their creation that the whole series of volitions of the mind answers, in the most perfect harmony, to the whole series of the motions of the body.

As the second system complicates rather than explains the difficulty, we must reject it.

The fourth system does not differ from the third

in regard to the present difficulty, which is to determine whether there is a mutual influence of the soul and the body on each other. Both systems deny that there is any such influence, and in this respect they do not differ, although in other respects they differ greatly. In each, however, especially in that of Leibnitz, we do not see how human freedom would be safe.

There remains the first system, shall we admit the existence of a real mutual influence, a true causality, between the soul and the body; or, according to the third system, a mere occasionality? That there is a real influence we propose to prove by the following

Proposition.—*The soul has a direct influence upon the body, and the body upon the soul.*

Argument: If the existence of this mutual influence is not shown to be impossible, and if it is even proved by many facts that the influence does exist, then the proposition must be accepted as true; but such is the case, and hence the soul has a direct influence, &c.

Proof: 1st. It has never been shown that the existence of this influence is impossible. When we say that the soul can act directly upon the body, we do not mean that it acts materially, for it is a spiritual substance; but we mean that the soul has a natural power of moving the body. That the existence of this power of spirit over matter is not impossible is evident from the fact that God, who is a pure spirit, does move material substances.

That the influence of the body upon the soul is a

passive one is evident from the fact that the body, being matter, is inert of itself. The body is like an instrument in the hands of a workman; it acts, or has influence, upon his will in proportion to its degree of fitness and perfection. Besides, it has not been shown that the forces of attraction and repulsion, existing among the molecules of matter according to the arrangement made by God, do not exercise some action or influence upon the soul.

2nd. Many facts and circumstances prove the mutual influence of the body and the soul. These facts are:

(a) *The testimony of consciousness.* Whenever I move my body I am conscious, not only of my will to move my body, but even of a certain effort of the soul to move it, and I clearly perceive that the movement of my body responds to the effort of my soul.

(b) *The universal persuasion of mankind.* All men are convinced that the human will is the moving cause of bodily action, and also that the body reacts upon the soul. This testimony, as we have proved, is a sufficient argument to establish certitude.

(c) *The unity of human personality.* Personality, in man, is a union between the soul and the body, so complete that they form one individual who attributes to himself all the actions of the soul and the body, who can say with equal correctness, *I* think and *I* walk. It is clear that we could not thus express ourselves if we did not know and feel that our actions are indeed our own, and not the result of the actions of God in consequence of the volitions of our mind or the movements of our body.

(d) *The power which the mind has of directly perceiving corporeal objects.* This has been established in *Logic*, in treating of the evidence of the senses. The existence of this power shows that the senses have a direct influence upon the soul. The first system may therefore be now considered as fully proved to be the true one.

NOTES.—(1) Philosophers have examined the question concerning the origin of the soul. It is clear, and also generally admitted, that souls are created immediately by God, without the co-operation of parents; and, consequently, the soul does not exist before the conception of the body, for this pre-existence, which is contrary to the teaching of theology, seems entirely opposed to reason and to the wisdom of God.

(2) In regard to the consequences of the union of the body with the soul, there are two kinds of phenomena; the first ones are the result of the influence of the body upon the mind, as has been noticed in *Experimental Psychology*, in treating of sensation, memory, &c., when both soul and body are in a normal condition, and in treating of delirium, &c., when they are in an abnormal condition; and the others are the result of the influence of the mind upon the body, as it has been said in treating of the changes of the voice, countenance, &c., when we wish to show the feelings of the soul, in other words, when the influence of the soul is exercised upon the body.

CHAPTER THIRD.

Of the Destiny of the Soul.

It has been shown that the soul and the body are two substances, entirely distinct and different. The dissolution of the body does not involve that of the soul, since the soul is not divisible, that is, is not composed of parts. The dissolution of the body does not necessitate the annihilation of the soul; for if such were the case it would be because the soul could not exercise her faculties without the body, but this is not so, for there are in the soul many faculties which by their nature have no connection with the body: such are the faculties of thinking, judging, reasoning, &c. Hence we may conclude that the soul may outlive the body. This property of the soul is its immortality.

Since the soul may outlive the body, there must be another life; at least, the above remarks will justify us in concluding that the existence of another life is possible. Does this life then exist? This question properly belongs to *Ethics*, and we shall only consider it briefly in this place.

The existence of another life is rendered necessary, 1st, by two attributes of God, His justice and His wisdom. 2nd. It is shown by the desire born with us to enjoy a felicity not to be found here, and which must be found somewhere. 3d. It is proved by the natural inclination of men to seek for reputation, glory and immortality. 4th. It is proved by the common consent of mankind, who have always in their treatment of the dead shown their conviction of the existence of another life. It cannot be objected to this that the testimony of a good conscience, or the hope of reward, are a sufficient sanction to the natural law; for experience shows that a time comes for some men when these impressions are of no avail. 5th. It is proved by the consequences which would be the result of the contrary belief.

NOTE.—The eternal duration of the other life is not in contradiction to reason.

CHAPTER FOURTH.

OF THE SOULS OF ANIMALS.

Besides God, the angels and the human soul, there is the inferior soul of animals. By this soul we mean the principle by which the animal has its life. Let us examine, first, what are the faculties of this soul, and, second, what is its nature and destination.

ARTICLE FIRST.—THE FACULTIES OF THE SOULS OF ANIMALS.

We find in those animals that have the most perfect organization these faculties, sensibility, intellect and activity.

(a) *Sensibility.* Animals have (1) a physical sensibility which is superior in acuteness to that of man, as that of sight in the eagle. They have (2) physical appetites as men have. (3) In some of them we find desires and passions, as the inclination to live in society, emulation, ostentation, envy

METAPHYSICS. 171.

and avariciousness. (4) We find in some animals affections, that is sentiments either good or bad.

(b) *Intellect.* The degree of intellect is not the same in the different classes of animals. The mammals have the greatest amount of intellect. They are found to possess the following faculties: (1) By the organs of sense they perceive certain qualities of many bodies placed before them; and this perception produces a conviction which excludes any doubt, as in the case of oats placed before a horse. Hence (2) they have consciousness of their own sensations and operations. (3) They are capable of being attentive, as a hunting dog scenting game. (4) They have memory. A horse will after years recognize a road through which he has once passed. (5) Some animals have imagination; and this is the only way of explaining their dreams. (6) Many animals have the power of expressing themselves exteriorly, or of communicating their sentiments. (7) It would not be unreasonable to admit in them something more than attention, in fact a sort of calculation on their part, in order to explain some extraordinary phenomena.

(c) *Activ'ty.* Some of the actions of animals are spontaneous and others voluntary; some proceed from instinct, some from choice, and others again from acquired habits.

Instinct in animals takes the place of reason; certain actions of theirs, as we have said, proceed from choice, as, for instance, a dog will abstain from food for fear of a stick with which he is threatened.

The difference between men and the inferior animals is (1) that men are endowed with reason, which belongs to the nature of the human soul; consequently, by their nature men are superior. It is by reason that men distinguish what is good, true, beautiful, &c., and it is certain that the lower animals cannot make these distinctions. (2) The lower animals are incapable of morality: having no moral liberty, their actions are not characterized by moral good or malice.

ARTICLE SECOND.—THE NATURE AND DESTINY OF THE SOULS OF ANIMALS.

It is evident that there is in all animals some immaterial substance. We must believe this (1) since they exhibit activity, sensibility, and phenomena indicating an inferior intellect; and (2) since these phenomena allow us to conclude in favor of the existence of a substance which is active, sensible and has an inferior intellect; and (3) since such substance ought to be immaterial.

(1) We have seen in the first Article that animals show signs of activity, etc.

(2) We may conclude from the existence of these signs or phenomena, what we logically concluded concerning the human soul, namely, the existence of a substance which is active, sensitive and intelligent.

(3) This substance must be essentially immaterial, since these faculties are essentially different from the properties found in matter.

We may therefore reject the doctrine of Descartes, who says that beasts are mere machines, and also the doctrine of some modern dreamers, called philosophers, who pretend that men are not superior to beasts.

The soul of the inferior animal cannot of course be dissolved by the dissolution of its body, since it is an immaterial substance; but as there is no reason for admitting the existence of another life for such souls, we may consider as reasonable the opinion of those who think that such substances are annihilated as soon as their services are no longer needed.

PART III.

ETHICS; OR, MORAL PHILOSOPHY.

ETHICS;

OR,

MORAL PHILOSOPHY.

THE words *Ethics* and *Morals* have the same meaning: the first comes from the Greek ιθος, and the second from the Latin *mores*.

Ethics is the practical science which directs human actions toward honesty.

Human actions are those which we perform as human beings, that is, with the knowledge of the intellect and the consent of the will. Actions performed without this knowledge or consent are called the *actions of man (actus hominis)*.

We have already said, in *Ontology*, that there exists in the world a two-fold order, the physical and the moral.

Beings deprived of their liberty necessarily follow the order assigned them by their Creator; so that if there is disorder, the disorder cannot be attributed to them as the cause thereof: consequently they deserve neither praise nor blame.

Beings endowed with liberty are responsible for their actions; according to their own wish, they follow or refuse to follow the order assigned them: and this is the first principle of human actions.

Human actions may be considered both in general and in particular; hence the division of this Part into two dissertations.

FIRST DISSERTATION.

ON HUMAN ACTIONS IN GENERAL.

Human actions are considered in general when they are examined abstractly, that is, the special state of man being laid aside.

We have first to examine whether there are actions which are good and others which are bad, also what is the source of each and how we may make a distinction between them. Hence the division of this dissertation into three chapters; in the first of which we shall treat of the difference between good and bad actions, in the second of the principles of these actions, and in the third of the rules marking distinctions between them.

CHAPTER FIRST.

Of the Difference Between Good and Bad Actions.

It would be useless to give rules of conduct if there were no difference between good and evil. We must consequently first determine whether there is such a difference, and if so whether there is any natural obligation of doing good and avoiding evil. In order to proceed methodically we shall divide this chapter into five articles. In the first we shall examine whether there is any difference between good and evil; and in the second, whether there is an obligation to do good and avoid evil, that is, whether there is a natural law: in the third we shall establish the fact of the promulgation of that law; in the fourth we shall prove that the law is immutable; and in the fifth we shall show what is its sanction.

ARTICLE FIRST.—THE DIFFERENCE BETWEEN MORAL GOOD AND MORAL EVIL.

This difference has been denied by Epicurus and his disciples, by Hobbes and Spinosa, and by the modern deists, as Helvetius, La Mettrie and d'Holbach. Their principles are, first, that man has received no useless faculties from nature, and consequently that what is possible to him is also lawful for him; and, second, that, in order to obtain security for themselves, men made an agreement to abstain from actions which might be injurious to the general welfare, from which, they say, resulted the distinction between good and evil.

But we affirm that there is an essential difference between good and evil, as there is an essential difference between truth and falsehood; and, to prove this, we will establish the following

Proposition.—*Moral good and moral evil are essentially different.*

I. We prove this proposition first by its own evidence. What the mind clearly perceives as existing does really exist. But we clearly perceive the difference spoken of in the proposition; it therefore does exist. For instance, the mind clearly perceives that it is right to honor our parents and wrong to insult them. The knowledge of this difference being a primary truth, its existence cannot be directly demonstrated.

II. In the second place, we prove this truth by the unanimous consent of mankind. That this consent exists we may know by daily experience, by the annals of all nations and by the language of every people. We may moreover prove it by the manner of acting of those whose advantage it would be to deny the existence of this difference. There is not a wicked person who would not like to call his bad actions good, if he could do so; and the very fact that he tries to do it shows that he admits that there is a difference between good and evil. The remorse which he feels is the best evidence of the truth of the proposition. It may further be proved by the manner of acting of those who deny theoretically the existence of the difference; for these same deists, like all men, praise virtue and condemn vice. Since then this general consent exists, since it concerns a matter of great importance, and since it is in opposition to our passions, it must be an infallible motive of certitude. As we have said in *Logic*, such a consent could not come from education, prejudice or agreement; it must therefore come from nature, and is consequently the expression of truth.

III. Thirdly, we prove this proposition by noting the absurd consequences of the opposite doctrine. If this difference did not exist, then good and evil would be the same; but this is in contradiction to the common sense of men and their practices in daily life. If this difference is not essential, but the result of an agreement, it would follow that to-morrow men might agree that it is right to insult our parents and wrong to honor them, which is evidently absurd. Hence we conclude that there is an essential difference between good and evil, that this difference is based upon the essence of things and upon the first principles of morals, and that neither God nor man could alter them.

The principles of morals are of course the same for all men. However, in regard to the application of these principles we find a great diversity of opinion; and, in regard to their remoter consequences, even the most learned men do not agree. All peoples, for instance, know that it is right, and even obligatory on us, to honor our parents; yet nations are found where men think it an act of kindness to kill their parents when they become very old. The love of parents for their children has also been strangely abused by those who, through fear of future want or misery, think it allowable to kill their own offspring. Objections to our proposition may be answered by the aid of these remarks.

ARTICLE SECOND.—THE OBLIGATION OF DOING GOOD AND AVOIDING EVIL, OR THE EXISTENCE OF THE NATURAL LAW.

The word law is probably derived from *ligare*, to bind. A *law* is a precept which is common to all, just, stable, given by a superior, sufficiently promulgated and sanctioned.

Law is a precept, and not an advice; common to all

and consequently different from a mandate, which is made for certain persons; just, for no one can command that which is unjust; stable, because it is not a transitory act, permanence being essential to it; sufficiently promulgated, for it must be made known, and this can be done only by promulgation; given by a superior, a legitimate superior only having the power to command and to exact obedience; sufficiently sanctioned; for otherwise the superior could not realize his end.

There is no superior unless there are subjects.

The power to command supposes the obligation of obedience.

The obligation of obedience to law is not deduced from human reason, considered in itself, but from the supreme dominion of God. The obligation of obedience to a law cannot be deduced from the human reason considered absolutely; because, in order to impose an obligation, two wills are necessary, the one of a superior having a right to command, and the other of an inferior who is bound to obey: but the human will, considered abstractly from God, is not that of a superior, all men being naturally equal; hence the human will cannot create an obligation. The obligation must therefore come from the authority of God; and when a man commands he does so as holding the place of God: *omnis auctoritas a Deo*, all authority proceeds from God.

Consequently, according to the Atheists there could be no obligation of obedience.

From all eternity, God sees the supreme order of the essence and relations of things. This order constitutes the law which is called moral, when considered in reference to free and intelligent beings; and the disturbance of this same order constitutes moral evil.

The supreme reason existing in God, determining in a fixed manner what may be done and what may not be done, is called the eternal law. The eternal law is therefore the will of God commanding the maintenance and forbidding the disturbance of the natural order of things.

The natural law is a participation of the eternal law by rational creatures. We may define it to be a precept by which God commands us to fulfill the duties which arise from the nature of things; the necessity of which our reason may know, either by itself, or by the aid of another being.

Proposition.—*There exists a natural law.*

I. We might first give as an evidence of this truth several passages of the Holy Scripture, quoted or found even in the writings of pagans, as that of Psalm xxxiii—15, *Diverte a malo et fac bonum*, avoid evil and do good.

II. We have seen that there exists in the world a supreme order, but it is impossible to admit that God does not take care to have that order respected and observed by his free creatures: to admit that God looks with indifference on all our actions would be to deny his wisdom, his sanctity, etc.

III. If we except the Epicureans, we find that the legislators and the peoples of all ages have believed that God regards the actions of men, in order to reward the good and punish the wicked; and we know that such a consent is an infallible motive of certitude.

Article Third.—The Promulgation of the Natural Law.

I. There is no one having the use of reason who does not perceive within himself the presence of a light by the aid of which he can discern good from evil, and judge surely that some of his actions are right and others wrong. This light, found in the minds of all men, must come from God, the author of nature, and must therefore be the means of showing us what is his will. Thus the natural law is made manifest to us, and this manifestation is its promulgation, and creates for us an obligation of obedience. No form is required for such promulgation: it is sufficient for us that the will of God has been made known to us.

In the same manner the first precepts of morals are made evident to our souls. However, this light, which is merely rational, is exceedingly feeble in some men, and in others it is almost obscured, especially concerning several consequences deduced from first principles. In order to help our natural weakness God has further enlightened our minds by revelation, by the authority of the Church and by tradition.

To conclude, we may say that conscience, even when aided by education, could not discover many things which by deduction belong to the natural law: it is therefore no wonder that many philosophers, not enlightened by revelation, have given forth so many absurd and even monstrous systems.

II. It has been a question whether, in the present state of things, there can be an invincible ignorance of the natural law. By invincible ignorance is understood such an ignorance as cannot be removed by the ordinary help of nature and grace. The contrary is called vincible ignorance. Some rigid doctors, chiefly of the University of Louvain, have contended that there can be no invincible ignorance even of the most remote consequences of the violation of the natural law; because, they contend, these consequences are essentially bad, and no one can be invincibly ignorant of what is essentially wrong.

This opinion is generally rejected. We know that this invincible ignorance exists, since we see the most learned doctors, as St. Thomas and St. Bonaventure, giving contradictory solutions to questions resting on the natural law. But concerning the primary precepts of the natural law and the proximate conclusions deduced from them, there is of course no invincible ignorance in any man with the use of his reason.

III. The judgment of the mind concerning the morality of an action performed or about to be performed by it is called the conscience. Hence in Ethics we do not consider the conscience merely as a faculty, but also as an action.

As this subject belongs to theology we shall here content ourselves with a few general remarks.

Conscience is either true or false, certain or doubtful.

A true conscience is one which declares lawful or

unlawful that which really is so; a false one being, of course, the contrary.

A certain conscience is one which judges prudently, and without any fear of probable error, that some action is good or bad. Hence we may see that a certain conscience may not be a true one; such a conscience, when in error, is said to be invincibly erroneous.

A doubtful conscience is one which abstains from judging, because it perceives on both sides opposing reasons.

1st. It is plain that a true, or at least a certain, conscience must be the rule of all our actions.

2nd. It is never allowable for us to act against our conscience, even if it should afterwards appear that our conscience was is error; for to act against our conscience is to be willing to commit sin..

ARTICLE FOURTH.—THE IMMUTABILITY OF THE NATURAL LAW.

The immutability of the natural law consists in this, that what is declared good by the natural law can never become bad, and *vice versa*.

Proposition.—*The natural law is immutable*.

This is proved, first, by the intrinsic goodness of certain actions, and the intrinsic badness of others.

Certain actions, as the honor due to God, are perceived by us to be so intrinsically good, and others are perceived to be so intrinsically bad, that never, in any hypothesis, can they be otherwise. Hence the law which commands us to observe this necessary order is immutable.

In the second place, the moral axioms, or the first principles of the natural law, are necessary truths, just as the mathematical axioms are necessary truths. The principle "We must give to every one what belongs to him," is as necessarily true and immutable as the axiom "The whole is equal to the sum of its parts." Hence the natural law is immutable, and can suffer neither dispensation nor derogation.

Some facts of Holy Scripture have been quoted against the truth of this proposition; as the command of God to Abraham to kill his son, and to the Israelites to take the vessels of the Egyptians. In the first there was no violation of the natural law, for this law forbids us to inflict death on our fellowmen by private authority; but God, being the supreme master of our lives, may, in virtue of his divine authority, command any one for a just cause to take away the life of another. In the case of the Egyptians, the Hebrews merely took back what was their own. In neither case therefore was there any dispensation or abrogation of the natural law.

ARTICLE FIFTH.—THE SANCTION OF THE NATURAL LAW.

By the *sanction* of the natural law, we understand the reward bestowed on those who observe the law, and the punishment inflicted on those who violate it. In regard to this sanction we proceed to prove the following propositions:

First Proposition.—*God has established a sanction for the natural law.*

God being infinitely wise and powerful, has taken the proper means to secure the observation of the laws which he has established. But, considering the natural disposition of men, it is evident that a sanction is necessary for the enforcement of the natural law; for if left to his own inclinations man will not obey unless he forces himself, and he will not force himself unless he is compelled to do so: for this compulsion duty is not always a sufficient motive; rewards and punishments must be provided. Hence God must have established a sanction for the natural law.

Second Proposition.—*The natural law has some sanction even in this world, but this sanction is incomplete and even void if separated from the sanction of another life.*

1st. The natural law has some sanction even in this world, that is, some reward is bestowed on those who observe the law, and some punishment is inflicted on those who violate it; for experience shows that virtue makes a man happy, so far as it is possible to be happy in this world, and, on the contrary, that vice makes him unhappy.

2nd. This sanction, in the present life, is incomplete; because it is not in strict proportion to the merit of virtue or the demerit of vice; and because, as we all know, there are many virtuous actions that have no reward in this world, and many vicious ones that receive no punishment.

3d. Moreover this sanction, in the present life, is almost void if separated from the sanction of the future life. Virtue makes one happy because it brings peace of conscience, and vice renders one unhappy because it is followed by remorse of conscience;

but if we remove the certitude of another life this peace and this remorse would have no real foundation.

All admit, when they speak seriously, that the desire of enjoying a good name among men, the intrinsic beauty of virtue, and the deformity of vice, are not sufficient motives for securing the observance of the natural law.

We may conclude, from these considerations, that there is another life; and that that life will be eternally happy for the good, for God can never cease to love them; and eternally unhappy for the wicked, this eternity of punishment not being repugnant to the justice, wisdom or goodness of God. This last conclusion, concerning the eternal duration of rewards and punishments, has always been believed by the generality of mankind.

NOTE.—It is worthy of inquiry whether one who observes the law on account of its sanction, that is, on account of the hope of reward or the fear of punishment, performs a good moral action.

We must distinguish: 1st. He who abstains from evil on account of mere hope or fear, but retains the desire to do evil if the sanction were removed, does not perform a good action, because his will is evil. 2nd. He who observes the law, on account of the hope of reward or the fear of punishment, but also with the desire of thus doing his duty, performs a good action, for he does good on account of the duty resting upon him. 3d. He who observes the law on account of the hope of reward or the fear of punishment, without considering the question of right or duty, does not indeed perform a bad action; but his action is less perfect than that of the man who acts on account of duty.

CHAPTER SECOND.

Of the Principles of Good and Bad Actions.

These principles are the sources of goodness and wickedness; they are, the intellect, liberty and the will.

1st. It is certain that in order that an action be good or bad, it is necessary the intellect should know it to be such before it is performed. An act done without the knowledge of the intellect is not a human action.

2nd. It is also certain that liberty in the actor is necessary for the morality of a human action. If the actor is not free, the act cannot be considered his own. An act done through necessity must be charged, not to the agent, but to the cause which determined him to act.

3d. Again, it is certain that the will only is the cause and the foundation of sin; as it is also the cause and the foundation of virtue. The will, understood in this sense, is consequently human liberty in exercise.

The will considered in the act, is either simple or free. Its operation is called volition.* Volition is itself either simple or free. It is simple when there is knowledge of the intellect and consent of the will;

---

* This word means here what the authors express by *voluntarium*.

it is free when besides these two there is also deliberation. Hence what is free is voluntary, but what is voluntary is not necessarily free. For instance, we seek our happiness voluntarily, but not freely. It is free volition only which is the principle of our actions.

Volition is direct when something is positively and in itself intended by the agent; and indirect when something is willed, not in itself, but in the cause of which it is the effect. For instance, if one burst a shell for mere amusement, and thus accidentally kill a man, he does not will the death of the man directly but indirectly.

Volition is perfect if it does not suppose any repugnance of the will, otherwise it is imperfect. An example of imperfect volition is that of a merchant at sea who throws his goods overboard for fear of shipwreck.

The causes which may diminish or destroy the freedom of the will are: force, fear, error, ignorance and passion.

CHAPTER THIRD.

RULES FOR DISTINGUISHING GOOD FROM BAD ACTIONS.

It is clear that we must avoid everything which is bad, but that we are not obliged to do everything which is good, as this latter would be impossible. Hence, the precept to avoid evil is negative and universal, whereas the command to do good is affirmative and particular. The first obliges always and in all cases; while the second obliges always, but not in all cases. The questions which belong to this chapter are all theological, and are fully examined in the treatise on "Human Actions."

SECOND DISSERTATION.

ON HUMAN ACTIONS IN PARTICULAR.

Man, as a moral agent, may be considered in three points of view, in his relations with God, with himself and with his fellow-men. Hence the three varieties of his special duties.

Duty means the same as obligation. It is a moral restriction of the natural powers of a person. This is called a moral restriction, because duty imposes not a physical, but a moral restraint.

This restriction is the result of the power which one being has either of doing something without hindrance from another being, or of exacting something from that other being: this last power is called *right*. Hence right is the cause or origin of duty; they are correlative, and one cannot exist, or be conceived, without the other.

Right is then the lawful authority of one being to do something, or to exact something of another being. From this definition, it is easy to conceive how duty results from right: First, if a being has lawful authority to act in a certain manner, all other beings are bound not to impede his action; and, second, if a being has lawful authority to exact an action from another being, that other being is bound to perform the required action.

The duties of men are of three kinds, according to the division given above: duties towards God, towards themselves, and towards one another. There can be no other kind of duties, as, for instance, towards beings without reason; for such beings can have no right, and hence there can be no obligation in regard to them.

CHAPTER FIRST.

Of the Duties of Men towards God.

The duties of men towards God, taken altogether, are called *worship*. Concerning this we have two questions to examine, 1st, Is man bound to worship God? and, 2nd, Did God supernaturally reveal to man the manner in which He must be worshiped?

This second question, which is theological, is fully discussed in the treatise "On Religion," in theology. Here we have to examine only the first question, which we shall do by establishing the necessity of religious worship, and by giving the causes which induce men either to neglect or to corrupt that worship.

Article First.—The Necessity of Religious Worship.

Worship is both interior and exterior. Interior worship is the sum of all our duties towards God, in so much as they consist in certain interior acts of the mind, as to love, to submit our will to the will of God, etc. Exterior worship is the outward manifestation of our interior worship; and is itself either private or public. Private worship is that paid to God by men in their own name; and public worship is that rendered to God by men as members of society.

Concerning the necessity of religious worship, as thus explained, we establish the following propositions:

First Proposition.—*Man is bound to give interior worship to God.*

Man is bound to act towards God in accordance with the attributes of God and man's own condition; and both of these require an interior worship of man towards God.

1st. The attributes of God. God is infinitely perfect, and must therefore be loved by his creatures; he has supreme dominion over all things, and must therefore be adored: but love and adoration are both acts of interior worship.

2nd. The condition of man. Man having been created by God, is obliged in return to give to him, as to his last end, all his actions and even his being itself; having been the object of the divine favor, he is obliged to return thanks to God; and being in need of divine assistance, he is obliged to ask the help of God: but the direction of our actions towards God, thanksgiving for favors and petitions for help, are all acts of interior worship. Hence the proposition.

Interior worship consists, first, in loving, for love being the noblest faculty of the soul is also the first; and second, in obeying, for obedience is the proof of our love. Besides these duties, adoration, offering one's self to God, thanksgiving and prayer are so many acts of interior worship.

Second Proposition.—*Man is obliged to render to God an exterior worship.*

This proposition may be proved, first, by the necessity there is for this worship, in order that we may be assured of the reality of our interior worship; for man cannot feel deeply without showing what he feels by some exterior signs. Hence, where there is no exterior worship there may be doubt whether there is any interior.

It may be proved, in the second place, by the necessity of exterior worship for the preservation of the interior. Experience shows that the sense of religion is not long retained in our mind unless it is stirred and warmed, as it were, by exterior signs.

Thirdly, exterior worship is necessary, because it is the tribute paid by our body to God, as interior worship is the tribute of the soul. Both owe worship to God, who is the author of both soul and body.

Third Proposition.—*Man is bound to give public worship to God.*

This proposition is proved by these two considerations: 1st. Public worship is necessary for the preservation of both interior and exterior worship; experience shows the truth of this, especially in the case of ignorant and uncultivated persons. 2nd. Public worship is the tribute due to God by the moral body called society; and, besides, society, as a body, having need of assistance, must seek it from God.

Fourth Proposition.—*The necessity of interior, exterior and public worship is proved by the unanimous consent of mankind.*

This is a fact which no one can deny; and this unanimous consent is an infallible motive of certitude. Cicero says: "Each state has its own religion;" and Plutarch: "No one has ever seen a place without worship."

Note.—The principal signs that constitute as it were the essence of exterior and public worship are: vocal prayer, singing, certain reverential motions and postures of the body, sacrifice and burning of incense.

When man frequently fulfills his duties to God he acquires an ease and pleasure in worship which soon becomes a habit. This habit is called piety, or a religious disposition.

Piety is therefore the virtue which inclines men to give to God the veneration and worship, both interior and exterior, which is his due. There is, however, a difference between piety and a disposition to fulfill our religious duties. This religious disposition is the state of mind of one who is unwilling to omit to render to God the worship which is due to him; while piety disposes one not only to render to God the worship which is due to him, but also to do this with fervor and great reverence.

Piety is both interior and exterior: the first is a habitual intercourse existing interiorly between God and the soul; the second consists in exterior practices of devotion. Piety is true and solid only when it is both interior and exterior. Solid piety is the most sure foundation of morality.

ARTICLE SECOND.—THE CAUSES WHICH INDUCE MEN EITHER TO NEGLECT OR TO CORRUPT THE WORSHIP OF GOD.

I. The causes that lead men to neglect divine worship are of two kinds: those that lead them to deny even in theory the necessity of divine worship, and those that induce them to omit this worship in practice. Of the first kind are atheism, and a false opinion of providence, as in the case of those who deny that God wants any worship, or that he cares for it. Of the second are indifference in matters of religion, very common as we all know, and the slavery of the passions; this slavery is very much opposed to the worship of God, as it is a true idolatry. Very many of these idolators are found in the world.

II. The causes that alter and corrupt divine worship are: idolatry, superstition, and lack of solid interior piety, that is, lip-worship instead of heart-worship. These causes corrupt not only divine worship, but also public morals. This is especially the case with idolatry: the pagan world furnishes a most shameful example of the fact.

CHAPTER SECOND.

OF THE DUTIES OF MAN TOWARDS HIMSELF.

These duties may be reduced to two: the obligation of preserving the life of the body, and that of cultivating the faculties of the mind.

ARTICLE FIRST.—THE OBLIGATION OF PRESERVING THE LIFE OF THE BODY.

To preserve his life man must avoid suicide, and not otherwise expose himself without sufficient cause to the danger of losing his life or his health.

I. *Suicide.*

Suicide is the act of a man who willingly and knowingly kills himself. We will first proceed to show that suicide is unlawful, and, secondly, that the arguments which are brought forward to justify it are futile.

First Proposition.—*Suicide is unlawful.*

That is unlawful which is contrary to the destiny intended for man upon earth, and which is opposed to the glory of God, to the good of society and to the natural propensities of men ; but such is suicide.

1st. Suicide is contrary to the destiny intended for man upon earth. The present life is a time of probation: this follows from the fact of human liberty, and that of the existence of another life. For, since man can do either good or evil, and consequently gain merit or demerit, and since he is destined for another life which will be eternally happy or eternally miserable, it is evident that the present life is a time of probation. That it is not lawful for a man, by his own authority, to diminish the time of this probation imposed by God, is also clear; because it must be unlawful for a creature to oppose the end designed by his creator, and because it is essential to the nature of probation that its duration be not left to the choice of him who is in the state of probation, but rather of Him who has established the probation.

But by suicide a man diminishes the time of his probation, since he voluntarily deserts the station in which he has been placed by God. Hence suicide is, in the first place, contrary to the destiny intended by his Creator for man upon earth.

2nd. Suicide is opposed to the glory of God, since man by continuing to practice virtue glorifies God, whereas if he commits suicide he voluntarily refuses to serve God and thus opposes himself to the promotion of God's glory.

Suicide is also opposed to the good of society; for if suicide were declared lawful there is no doubt that many would persuade themselves that it would be better for them to die, and thus-numbers of useful members would be cut off from society.

Suicide, finally, is opposed to the natural propensities of men: it is opposed to common sense, for all men admire and esteem those who are patient and resigned in the sufferings of this life; it is opposed to our instinctive love of life, and this love being acknowledged by all men must be the voice of nature, which it is unlawful for us to disobey.

Observation.—Suicide is a most cruel act to one's self, since it hurls him headlong into the midst of the greatest calamities. He who is guilty of this crime dies in the actual commission of a bad action, and consequently puts it out of his power to make any atonement for the wrong which he does. His fate is the most deplorable that can befall a human being.

Second Proposition.—*The arguments in favor of suicide are futile.*

This proposition is a corollary of the first: if suicide be unlawful, then all arguments in its favor must be vain. We shall, however, completely expose the fallacy of all these arguments. Some declare that suicide is lawful, because, they say, life is a gift which we can renounce; others pretend to believe it an act of courage; others, again, affirm that it is a right of nature; and others, finally, would persuade us that it is an act quite indifferent in its character.

First reason: That life is a gift of God which we may renounce whenever it is useless to us and to others, and, *a fortiori*, whenever it becomes an intolerable burden.

Life is not a mere gift, granted without any condition and to be renounced whenever we please. By the very fact of our existence we are bound to serve God, not as we will, but as He wills; and, consequently, as long as He keeps us in this life, we must serve Him, and we are never allowed to change, by our own will, that way of serving him, by passing into another life. Hence we cannot lawfully renounce the gift of our own existence.

Nor is life ever useless to man. Whatever be his condition he can always make himself more and more worthy of that future beatitude for which this present life is a preparation.

Nor even when life seems to be an intolerable burden is it allowed to man to take it away. Whatever be the sufferings which make life seem intolerable, they can never constitute a motive for committing suicide; on the contrary, the greater the trials of this life the better are they to enable us to reach the end for which we have been destined, and indeed life, in order to be a probation, must be burdensome.

Besides, it is not true that life is ever entirely intolerable; for the trials of life are never so great that man may not bear them, provided he has firm confidence in God. The examples of many good persons have amply proved this in their sufferings. If therefore one who does not believe in the existence of Providence finds himself unable to bear the ills of this life, he cannot bring forward his unbelief as a lawful cause for committing suicide.

Second reason: That suicide is lawful and praiseworthy because it is an act of courage.

Such was the assertion of the Stoics; but it is not true, for the man who kills himself because he cannot bear his trials does not perform a courageous act, but a cowardly one, as even the pagans themselves acknowledged.

Third reason: That suicide is a natural right, as J. J. Rousseau and other deists have pretended.

This is false, since men cannot have received from nature a right which is in opposition to the design which their Creator had in view, namely, as we have seen, that this life should be a time of probation. Suicide is opposed to this design of God, and hence cannot be a natural right.

Fourth reason: That suicide is an act indifferent in its character, as Montesquieu, Voltaire, and the Encyclopedists have affirmed, since, says Montesquieu, suicide does not disturb the order established by divine Providence.

We have shown, in our answer to the third reason and elsewhere, that suicide does disturb the order established by Providence, since it is opposed to the end designed by God; hence it is not an indifferent act.

From the answers given above, we may conclude, first, that it is not lawful to kill one's self in order to avoid a more cruel death, and, secondly, that it is not lawful to commit suicide even in order to avoid the danger of committing sin, for to him that confides in God the occasion of sin is never insurmountable.

II. *Danger of Losing Life or Health.*

1st. It is clear that we are not permitted to expose our life when there is not a good reason for so doing, which reason must be of equal gravity with the danger incurred. Consequently, it is not lawful to expose our life for mere amusement.

2nd. It is clear, on the other hand, that it is lawful for us to expose ourselves to a probable or a certain danger of death, provided there is a reasonable cause for so doing, the gravity of the cause being in proportion to that of the danger. We may expose our life in order to obtain a greater good, as for the welfare of the State, or to preserve the life of another.

3d. It is further clear that such exposure of life is not only lawful but even praiseworthy.

4th. And, finally, it is clear that sometimes it is not only lawful and praiseworthy, but even obligatory for us to expose ourselves to certain danger of death. This is always the case in reference to our duties; for instance, a soldier must keep his post at any risk, and a priest must attend his sick parishioners, even when they are dying of pestilence.

Observation.—Although certain trades and occupations are unhealthy, or otherwise endanger life, yet on account of their general utility it is lawful to follow them, even though this utility be of mere temporary importance.

What we have said concerning the danger of losing life may also be applied to the danger of losing our health.

ARTICLE SECOND.—THE OBLIGATION OF CULTIVATING THE FACULTIES OF THE MIND.

Proposition.—*We are all obliged to cultivate and perfect the natural faculties and aptitudes of our mind.*

God gave us those faculties and aptitudes only that we might use them for promoting His glory and the good of ourselves and our fellow men. In order to promote the glory of God, we must cultivate the seeds of virtue which have been implanted in our heart; and in order to do good to ourselves and our fellow men, we must cultivate those aptitudes which we have received for following some occupation useful to mankind.

The faculties which we must cultivate are the intellect, the sensibility and the will.

(a) *Culture of the Intellect.*

The intellect is cultivated by the acquisition of

knowledge; and this knowledge may be necessary, useful or hurtful.

1st. *Necessary knowledge.* Every one should acquire that knowledge which is necessary to enable him to attain his end, in other words, that knowledge which concerns the general duties of men. These duties are nowhere so clearly pointed out as in the Christian doctrine. Every one should also apply himself to the study of those things which concern his special duties in life.

2nd. *Useful knowledge.* By useful knowledge is meant, not that which is necessary to enable us to discharge the duties of life, but that which may enable us to discharge these duties in a more perfect manner. But the acquisition of that knowledge which is only useful should never interfere with the acquisition of that which is necessary. A knowledge of the liberal arts and the sciences constitutes what may be called useful knowledge.

3d. *Useless or hurtful knowledge.* It is not lawful to waste our time in the acquisition of useless knowledge; and the acquisition of hurtful knowledge, such as may be had from the reading of bad books, is positively forbidden: for by such knowledge the intellect is weakened and corrupted, and we are prevented from attaining the end for which we have been placed in this world.

NOTE.—In order to acquire sound knowledge, we should, 1st, be careful not to study too many things at the same time; 2nd, with the assistance of some experienced person, we should choose the best books, and read them with the most serious attention; and,

3d, we should take particular notice of everything important which we come across in reading.

It has been made a question whether the study of the arts and sciences is hurtful to morals; and also whether it is profitable for people in general to engage in the study of the sciences and the liberal arts.

First question.—J. J. Rousseau, in a discourse delivered at Dijon, tries to show that the study of the arts and sciences corrupts good morals; and, consequently, of course, that this study does not improve the morals. Against these assertions, we establish the following

Proposition.—*The culture of the arts and sciences does not of itself corrupt the morals; on the contrary, this study exerts a powerful influence in favor of good morals.*

1st. That these studies do not corrupt the morals is evident from the fact that the arts and sciences are good in respect to their object, which object is the development of a series of truths from certain principles, or the expression of the beautiful in the physical and the moral order, or some other equally good and proper end; and the object being always thus proper and good, the study which has this object in view cannot be corrupting to the morals.

Experience also shows the falsity of Rousseau's assertion; for how many learned men are there whose honesty and purity of morals are as remarkable as their attainments in science.

Even Rousseau's own confession refutes him; for he has said in another discourse that he put forth the above paradox for the sake of vanity.

2ud. The culture of the arts and sciences even improves the morals. History shows that the ferocity of men has always been in proportion to their ignorance.

We have shown that of itself this culture does not corrupt morals: it may, however, do so incidentally; and hence we sometimes see learned men whose conduct instead of being virtuous is exceedingly vicious. These men abuse their knowledge, and the more learned they are the greater is the abuse of which they are guilty, according to the maxim: *corruptio optimi pessima*, (the worst corruption is that of the wise). But from this abuse of knowledge certainly nothing can be proved against knowledge itself, or against the culture of the arts and sciences.

It is objected against this proposition that the Egyptians, Greeks and Romans became wicked as they became more learned.

Intellectual culture had nothing to do with this, for the arts and sciences flourished in those countries long before the people became corrupt. Many examples may be given, on the other hand, of nations that became great and illustrious in consequence of the spread of knowledge among them; as the Franks under Charlemagne, the Italians under Leo X., &c.

It is said also that many ancient nations remained invincible so long as they remained ignorant; as the Persians, the Romans, &c. The inference that science caused the weakness of those nations is false; for it has not been proved that the study of science lessens the warlike spirit. And even supposing that such culture had weakened the courage of those peoples, we should still have to examine whether they were less happy after this warlike spirit declined than they had been while their heroism rendered them invincible: for, as the most courageous people are often the slaves of the lowest vices, it is certain that a warlike spirit alone is not sufficient to cause the other virtues to flourish in a nation.

Second question.—Whether it is profitable for people in general to engage in the study of the sciences and the liberal arts.

That it is profitable for all people to know how to read and write, and be acquainted with the common branches of knowledge, is something which we all know by experience. Reading especially is very useful to help them in the acquisition of the religious knowledge which is indispensable to them. But it may perhaps remain a question whether it is always profitable to children in humble circumstances to be instructed in those arts and sciences which will be of no service to them in the sphere of life in which they have been placed by Providence; for such studies generally serve only to disgust them with their condition, without enabling them to rise above it, unless indeed they are possessed of great natural talent.

(b) *Culture of the Sensibility.*

The various propensities of the sensibility may be reduced to two: love and hatred. The first was called by the ancients the concupiscible appetite, or the appetite of desire; and the second the irascible appetite, or the appetite of anger.

1st. Love should be directed towards the supreme good, and diverted from all bad or dangerous objects. The supreme good is God, and all created good must be loved for his sake, and in proportion to the degree of its perfection, or its approach to the supreme good.

Love should be diverted from every bad and dangerous object, that is, from everything which could prevent man from attaining his end. Among these dangerous objects are, bad books, most theatrical exhibitions, public balls, masks, etc.

2nd. Hatred must be overcome by the repression of the irascible appetite, so that it may not become a habit, which would be so much opposed to our own happiness and to the good of others. In order to correct this natural disposition to anger, which is the source of hatred, we should always think well of our neighbor's intentions and abstain from showing any external marks of ill-humor.

(c) *Culture of the Will.*

The will is the first and constitutive faculty of human morality. Its culture is of even more importance that of all the other faculties, since they serve only for the perfecting of the will. The culture and good use of the will consists in avoiding evil and doing good; and, consequently, this culture is the final object of the whole science of Ethics.

CHAPTER THIRD.

OF THE DUTIES OF MEN TOWARDS ONE ANOTHER.

The first question that presents itself in this connection is whether man was created for society, or not. When this has been answered we will consider the duties of men in their relations with society.

Society is the union of many persons for the purpose of attaining certain ends by their united efforts. Since society is threefold, domestic, civil and universal, we shall consider the different duties of men in reference to this threefold society.

Preliminary Article.—Destiny of man for the state of society, and consequences resulting from this state.

(A) Destiny of man for the state of society.

We here propose to give our chief attention to the refutation of Rousseau, who pretended to believe that man was not destined for the state of society, and that the state of society is actually hurtful to him, since it is the source of all the calamities and all the vices in the world.

Proposition.—*Man was born to live in society with his fellow men.*

Argument: Man was born for that state which is required by his propensities and his necessities; but his propensities and necessities demand that he should live in society with his fellows, and hence he was born for that society.

Proof: 1st. His propensities require the state of

society; for all men have a certain inclination to live in society, an inclination which we call the desire of society: now this propensity is natural to man, since it is found in every man and is inherent in the human mind itself. That this propensity is *universal* is evident from the fact that men have always lived in society. In the beginning, as soon as mankind became too numerous for the family form of government, they established among themselves a sort of public polity, by which the supreme authority was placed in the hands of one or more persons. From this fact, which is well established by history and tradition, we conclude that man was created to live in civil and political, as well as in domestic society. This propensity is inherent in the human mind; for experience shows that nothing is more tedious to man than solitude. Consequently, the propensities of man prove that he was born to live in society.

2nd. Man's necessities require the state of society. Domestic society is necessary for the development of man's intelligence and morality. A few examples of persons who have lived in the forests like wild beasts prove the truth of this assertion.

Civil society is necessary to man for the complete development of his faculties. To fully develop his aptitude for the cultivation of the arts and sciences, man must have imitation and emulation, which are to be found only in civil society. The wants of man therefore render society necessary to man, and consequently prove that he was born for society.

Principles to be observed in answering objections:

(a) The abuses sometimes found in society, as the tyranny of rulers and the slavery of those subject to them, do not prove that the state of society is injurious to man; because, first, these abuses are not essentially connected with society, since they are not found everywhere; and, secondly, the abuses of tyranny and servitude would be greater and more frequent in the savage state than they are in the state of civilized society.

(b) Sickness and other infirmities, which are sometimes said to be more frequent in a state of society than in a savage state, do not show that the state of society is hurtful to man; because, first, temperate and sober men, no matter where they live, are always in good health; and, secondly, although the dwellers in the wilderness are often stronger, they are not happier than those in civilized society, for happiness is found only in the development of all the powers of the body and the mind, especially those of the latter, which are but feebly developed in a savage state.

(B) Consequences resulting from the state of society.—Inequality of condition in life, and right of property.

Men cannot live in society with one another unless there be some inequality of condition among them, and unless the right to acquire and own property be recognized.

(a) Inequality of condition.

Here again we have to refute Rousseau, who taught that this inequality is an evil and contrary to natural right. This doctrine has been accepted and taught by St. Simon and his disciples who have labored to do away with every privilege of origin, condition, sex and nationality. To refute this system we propose the following

Proposition.—*Inequality of condition among men is not opposed to natural right.*

Argument: That which necessarily results from man's nature, and from his destiny to live in society, cannot be contrary to natural right; but such is the case with inequality of condition among men, hence this inequality is not opposed to natural right.

Proof: First, this inequality results from man's nature, since that nature subjects children to parents, the younger to the older, the weaker to the stronger, the ignorant to the learned, &c., and thus establishes unequal conditions among men; secondly, it results from the destiny of men to live in society; for no civil society can exist unless there be rulers and magistrates, the executors and defenders of the laws, which the citizens are bound to respect, and consequently unless there be among the citizens the inequality resulting from the necessary exercise of authority.

(b) The right of property.

We have already given the definition of *right*. The right of property, or property, is the lawful power of doing something or of requiring something to be done for our own benefit, and of preventing others from using that right. The things that form the object of property are either movable or immovable; that is, capable of being moved from place to place without serious injury, or incapable of such movement.

The right of property has been lately attacked by the Communists, whose system has been reduced to the following words: "La propriété c'est le vol," our property is whatever we wish to take. Against this false doctrine we establish the following

Proposition.—*The right of property is a lawful right.*

Argument: That is lawful which necessarily results from our activity, which has been acknowledged as lawful by all men, and which is necessary for the existence and well-being of society.

Proof: 1st. This right naturally flows from our activity; for when a man by his own activity and industry has improved some portion of matter which was not before occupied by another, he has, by that very fact, attached to the matter something which is his own, and which cannot be taken from him without depriving him of what is his, and consequently without injuring him. Hence the right necessarily results from our activity.

2nd. The lawfulness of the right of property has been acknowledged by all men. History shows this.

3d. Without this right domestic society is not possible. This society would be destroyed if parents could not feed, educate and provide for the livelihood of their children; but it is plain that they could not perform these duties if they had not the right of property, and consequently could not make donations, wills, &c.

4th. Civil society also is impossible without this right; for the industrious will cease to exert themselves as soon as they find that they have to divide the fruits of their toil with the lazy. Hence the truth of the proposition.

Corollary.—We may conclude that the right of property does not originate in civil authority, although this authority may direct and regulate it: civil authority should protect, but never destroy this right.

It is objected to the proposition that the soil is necessary for the exercise of human labor; and, consequently, that being thus necessary for the generality of mankind it cannot become the property of any particular man; and hence that no one can have any exclusive right to property.

The minor of this argument is false: for as soon as any one by his own labor has improved anything which was not before occupied, he has the right, as we have shown, to retain that thing as his own; otherwise he would be deprived of the fruits of his own labor. Nor can it be said that it is lawful to take property thus improved on account of the right which every one has to make use of some part of the earth: for we cannot admit that there can exist any right in opposition to another prior and well established right. Hence some part of the soil may become the exclusive property of one person.

DUTIES OF MEN IN THEIR RELATIONS WITH SOCIETY.

ARTICLE FIRST.—THE DUTIES OF MEN IN RELATION TO DOMESTIC SOCIETY.

Domestic society is the union of husband and wife, together with their children, besides servants and other immediate dependents, all forming one family. Domestic society is therefore threefold, conjugal, parental and *herile*.

(a) Conjugal society is that established between husband and wife by marriage. The first end of marriage is the birth of children, that the number of those who love and honor God may be thus increased. The second end of marriage is that each one may find in the society of a consort help and support in order to bear more easily the burdens of life. Two other ends, less perfect but not unlawful, may be added to these: marriage is contracted to enable each one to avoid more easily the sins of impurity; and also sometimes in order to have heirs to names, properties and dignities.

The choice of a partner for life should be attended with the greatest care: first, by asking light from God; secondly, by seeking the advice of parents; thirdly, by endeavoring to choose a person remarkable for piety and virtue; fourthly, by observing, as far as possible, a similarity of age, condition, fortune, &c.; and, fifthly, by being honest and truthful towards one another before the marriage is contracted.

The duties of married persons are: mutual love,

conjugal fidelity, mutual obedience, and mutual help.

(b) Parental society is that existing between parents and children, especially in reference to the education of the latter.

The duties of parents toward their children consist, first, in providing them food, raiment and shelter; second, in teaching them the elements of the Christian doctrine and giving them habits of piety and morality; third, in giving them an education suitable to their condition and talents; and, fourth, in providing them with the means of making their own livelihood.

The duties of children towards their parents consist in honor, respect, love, obedience and assistance.

(c) *Herile* society is that existing between employer and employed, for their mutual advantage.

The duties of employers consist in treating those in their employ with humanity, kindness and justice; in keeping the contracts or agreements made with them; in watching over their moral conduct; and in giving them opportunities of attending to their religious duties.

The duties of servants to their masters consist in reverence, obedience and fidelity.

ARTICLE SECOND.—THE DUTIES OF MEN IN RELATION TO CIVIL SOCIETY.

We shall first make some general remarks concerning civil society, and then speak of the duties of men as members of this society.

I. Civil Society Considered in Itself.

(A) Nature and forms of civil society.

Civil society is an association of men living together under the same supreme power, in order to derive from it certain temporal advantages. By these last words civil is distinguished from spiritual society.

Civil society is threefold in form: monarchy, aristocracy and democracy; according as the supreme power resides in one man, in several citizens or in the whole people.

Monarchy (μονος ἀρχή) is the form of civil society in which the supreme power resides in one man, who is called king, emperor, &c. The monarchy is either elective or hereditary.

Aristocracy (ἄριστος κράτος) is the form of civil society in which the supreme power is in the hands of an order of citizens of high rank: when the number of those thus holding the supreme power is but few, we have what is called an oligarchy (ὀλίγος ἀρχή), but this word is generally used in a bad sense.

Democracy (δῆμος κράτος) is the form of civil society in which the supreme power is placed in the whole body of the citizens, certain classes, however, are often excepted.

Some forms are called mixed governments, as the limited monarchy, called also a constitutional government.

Every form of civil society has its own advantages, but also, on account of the passions of men, its disadvantages; and it may be said that no one form is equally suitable for all peoples.

(B) The supreme power in civil society.

By the supreme power in civil society is meant the power which governs that society without any subordination to another power residing in the same society.

The necessity of such a power is evident; but we must examine several questions in reference to it: (a) What are the characteristics and attributes of the supreme power in civil society, (b) what is the origin or foundation of this power, (c) by what means it is acquired, and (d) what are the causes for which it may be taken away.

(a) Characteristics and attributes of the supreme power.

This power must first be independent of any other authority residing in the same state, for otherwise it would not be supreme; and, second, it must be one, for otherwise there would be a perpetual struggle, and consequently civil war, anarchy and ruin.

The attributes proceed from the duties and rights which pertain to this society. They are of three kinds, legislative, judicial and executive: these attributes of framing laws, of pronouncing judgment, and of carrying laws and sentences into effect are incidental to the supreme power.

(b) Origin or foundation of the supreme power.

Whence originates this power of making laws and punishing those who do not obey them? Some say that it originates in the will of the people, who confer upon the magistrate the authority necessary for the exercise of his office. Others contend that this supreme power in civil society derives its authority from the will of God, who, having destined man for this society, has for this reason established supreme power, and attached to it the right to compel obedience. This latter opinion is the one entertained by the Christian philosophers; and, to prove it to be correct, we establish with them the following

Proposition.—*The supreme authority in civil society comes ultimately from God, and not from the people.*

(1) This authority does not come from the people: for, as we have before said, to create an obligation two wills are necessary, one of a superior and the other of an inferior; but the will of the people is not that of a superior, since all men are by nature equal; consequently, neither the will of one man nor that of several, considered abstractly from the will of God, can impose any obligation upon another man. Men may choose one man, or several men, to exercise the supreme authority; but they cannot confer any authority, since they have none.

(2) The supreme authority comes from God. Since God wills that all men should live in civil society, he must have established a supreme authority, for without this authority civil society cannot exist. God therefore wills that a supreme authority exist among men; hence he creates it, and it comes from him and not from the people.

(c) Means by which the supreme power is acquired.

This question is twofold: How was supreme power acquired in the beginning; and how is it acquired now, when society is formed and consolidated?

1st. Four opinions have been entertained concerning the manner in which supreme power was acquired in the beginning : The first of these is that authority was acquired by election; the second opinion is that the supreme authority in civil society is but an extension of the paternal authority; according to the third opinion, men wanting protection acknowledged themselves dependent on others more powerful than they were; the fourth opinion is that God intervened directly and thus established supreme authority.

The fourth opinion is brought forward gratuitously, and we reject it in like manner. The second and the third opinion, unless they be considered substantially the same as the first, may also be rejected; for acknowledgment of superiority and paternity does not of itself constitute supreme authority, or even the right to exercise this authority, unless an election take place, that is, unless the people choose their rulers; and this is the first opinion, which is the true one.

2nd. How may supreme authority be now acquired, that is when society is already formed?

Four means are considered lawful for such an acquisition: election, succession, victory in a just war, and prescription. The first three of these need no explanation. In regard to prescription it is held that a ruler who is at first a usurper may after a time and under certain circumstances exercise a lawful authority. The lawfulness of such authority is grounded on reason and the consent of the people.

Reason teaches that one who has for many years exercised supreme power, even though originally a usurper, ought not to be deprived of this power at the imminent risk of greater calamities. In such cases God will confer supreme authority, because the welfare of the people is the supreme law.

The consent of the people also shows the lawfulness of prescription: it is recognized everywhere now, and we find examples of it in almost every country.

(d) Causes for which supreme power may be taken from a ruler.

These are: first, abdication; second, expiration of the term of election or appointment; third, expulsion after defeat in an unjust war; fourth, revocation on the part of the appointing power; fifth, removal for causes provided for in the constitution, as was the case in some parts of Germany during the middle ages in regard to princes who forfeited their power on becoming heretics. Concerning these five causes there is no controversy.

But it has been made a question whether insurrection against constituted authority be a lawful cause for taking away supreme power from a ruler. Three opinions have been given in answer to this question. The first is that of J. J. Rousseau, who pretends that a people may revolt against their rulers and expel them for any cause whatever. Rousseau logically deduces this opinion from his system concerning the origin of power, but the consequence is as false as the premises. The second opinion is that of Suarez, Bellarmin and others, who say that in case of tyranny it is lawful to revolt against a ruler and expel him. A third opinion is held by Bossuet and others, who teach that it is never lawful to revolt against a ruler, however tyrannical his government may be. These two opinions may be defended; still it must be confessed that the opinion of Bellarmin, though more plausible in theory, is rather dangerous in practice, being fraught with fearful consequences.

II. *Duties of Men Considered as Members of Civil Society.*

(A) Duties of all citizens to their country: First, they must obey the laws; second, they should exert their talents for the good of their country, by following some occupation useful to society; third, they must contribute from their wealth to the support of the government (by taxes, &c.); and, fourth, when necessary, they must even sacrifice their life for their country.

(B) Duties of magistrates: First, they are bound in all their actions to aim at the good of civil society; second, they should strictly follow the dictates of justice, by bestowing offices and honors on the most deserving, by inflicting punishments in proportion to crimes and not tolerating any conduct opposed to the public welfare, and by refraining from wronging the people by granting injurious monopolies and from wronging foreign nations by unjust treaties or alliances. To these should be added two other duties: those placed in supreme power should become thoroughly acquainted with the science of government in all its departments, and above all they should always show a good example in all things.

(C) Duties of citizens towards their chief magistrates. These duties are respect and obedience to their authority; for, as we have seen, this authority comes from God.

Article Third.—Duties of Men Towards One Another.

These duties may be reduced to two: to do unto others as we would have them to do unto us, and not to do unto others what we would not have them do unto us. The first are positive duties and the others negative.

I. *Positive Duties.*

These may be named in the following order: First, we must love our fellow men, since we are all the children of God; and, second, we must do good to them, for idle charity is unavailing. The good works which we must perform for other persons are both spiritual and temporal.

A certain order should be observed in our charity. According to St. Bernard, the rule of charity is that those in most need should receive first. In other cases we should prefer those who are near to us in blood, friendship or religion. "True charity begins at home."

II. *Negative Duties—Duels.*

Negative duties are those that prescribe something to be avoided. We must avoid everything which may injure our neighbor, either in soul or in body.

We injure the souls of our fellow men by scandal; and we injure their bodies, first, by homicide, or by mutilating, wounding or striking them (but evidently there is no injustice in injuring, or even killing, an unjust assailant); second, by stealing from them or otherwise injuring their property; and, third, by injuring their good name.

Duels.—A duel is a private combat between two persons, according to a previous agreement, the place, time and arms, being also agreed upon. Against this unholy practice we establish the following

Proposition.—*Duelling is opposed to natural right.*

Natural right forbids us to kill another, or to expose our own life, without sufficient reason. But he who fights a duel endangers his own life and that of his adversary without sufficient reason. The reason given must be, for instance, to prove one's innocence, to avenge an injury, to preserve one's honor, or to show that one is courageous; but none of these reasons is a sufficient cause for engaging in a duel: for, first, the innocent one may be killed, and thus it may be made to appear that he is guilty; secondly, no one has a right by his private authority to avenge himself; thirdly, honor cannot be acquired by a duel, it is rather a mark of heroism, and consequently of honor, to bear injuries with patience; and, fourthly, true courage is shown by practicing patience, and by reserving the sacrifice of one's life for the acquisition of something preferable to life itself, as the safety of our family or our country.

Observation.—Duelling, which is forbidden by the natural law when undertaken by private authority, may become lawful when performed under the direction of the magistrate for the good of the state, as when David went forth from the army of Saul to challenge Goliath to mortal combat.

The Church forbids duelling under pain of separation from her communion.

To answer objections, let us observe that there are two kinds of honor, true and fictitious: true honor is that founded on virtue, and fictitious honor is that based upon the opinions of men. We must defend true honor, even at the risk of life; for virtue is preferable to life itself: but fictitious honor ought not to be preserved at the risk of life, for human glory is no virtue. True honor never requires a duel for its preservation; on the contrary it requires that duelling should be avoided.

Some persons object that no one is obliged to suffer the loss of his reputation. This is false: if fame among men cannot be preserved without violating natural right and divine law, let it perish.

They add also that sometimes, especially among soldiers, a duel cannot be avoided without serious inconvenience, and consequently that in such a case it is allowed. Again the consequent is false: no inconvenience can render that lawful which is wrong in itself and forbidden by the natural law.

They still add that he who refuses to engage in a duel lowers himself in his own estimation. This objection is not a serious one: such a man should modify his opinion of himself, for it is a false one; his error cannot make duelling lawful.

The above exposition of our duties is deemed sufficiently developed for a course of philosophy.

10*

Let us close by saying that it is not enough for us to know our duties, we must practice them; otherwise, our knowledge, being without good works, would only make us worse in the sight of God. With the help of God, let us endeavor to bring forth fruit by the practice of good works, so that being more wise we may be more virtuous.

CONTENTS.

Preface.................................... 3

INTRODUCTORY.

I.

Definitions of Words........................... 7
  A being—Existence—Possibility—Attributes—Essence and nature of a thing—Genus—Species—Individuals—Science—Art—Knowledge—Faith.

II.

Definitions of Philosophy....................... 10

III.

Divisions of Philosophy........................ 12

IV.

Argument..................................... 13

PART FIRST.—LOGIC.

Definition—Division........................... 17

FIRST DISSERTATION.—ON IDEAS.

Chapter First.

Of Ideas considered as existing in the mind.............. 19
    § I.—Division of Ideas.............................. 19
    § II.—Properties of Ideas........................... 20
    § III.—Operations of the mind in regard to Ideas...... 21

Chapter Second.

Of Ideas considered out of the mind....................... 22

SECOND DISSERTATION.—ON JUDGMENT.

Chapter First.

Of Judgment considered as existing in the mind.......... 23

Chapter Second.

Of Judgment considered as existing out of the mind...... 24
    § I.—Conversion of Propositions..................... 27
    § II.—Opposition of Propositions.................... 28

THIRD DISSERTATION.—ON REASONING.

Chapter First.

Of the Syllogism and its rules............................ 30

Chapter Second.

Of the different sorts of Syllogisms 34

Chapter Third.

Of the forms of argument other than the Syllogism....... 37

Chapter Fourth.

Of Sophisms.. 30

Chapter Fifth.

Of the sources of Sophisms.................................. 43

FOURTH DISSERTATION.—ON METHOD.

First Division, the Method of Invention 45
Second Division, the Method of Demonstration, or Dialectics 48

FIFTH DISSERTATION.—ON CERTITUDE.

Chapter First.

Preliminary notions—Definitions 50

Chapter Second.

Of the Criterion of Certitude............................... 52

Chapter Third.

Of the Existence of Certitude 55

Chapter Fourth.

Of the Motives of Certitude................................ 60
   1st Motive—The Certitude of pure reason 60
   2nd Motive—Consciousness 62
   3d Motive—The evidence of the senses................ 63
   4th Motive—The consent of mankind in things of the
      moral order...................................... 65
   5th Motive—The testimony of men.................... 67
     § I.—Authority of such testimony concerning natural
       facts... 69
     § II.—Authority of the same testimony concerning
       supernatural facts 72
   6th Motive—Memory 73
   7th Motive—Induction or analogy.................... 74
Appendix—Probability 76

PART SECOND—METAPHYSICS.

FIRST DISSERTATION.—ON ONTOLOGY.

Chapter First.

Of the notion, essence, possibility of a being in general.... 82

Chapter Second.

Of the causes and the effects of beings.................... 85

Chapter Third.

Of the different species of being......................... 89
    Article First.—Substance and modification............ 89
    Article Second.—Infinite and finite substances 91
    Article Third.—Material and spiritual substances...... 92

Chapter Fourth.

Of the properties of being............................... 93

Chapter Fifth.

Of space and time....................................... 97

SECOND DISSERTATION.—ON THEODICY.

PART FIRST.—THE EXISTENCE OF GOD.

Chapter First.

Of Atheism... 101
    § 1st.—Is it prudent to remain indifferent concerning the existence of God?..................... 101
    § 2nd.—Are there any evils resulting from the adoption of the theory of the Atheists?.............. 103
    § 3d.—Is Theism better than Atheism?......... 104
    § 4th.—Is Theism safer than Atheism?................ 104
    § 5th.—Is Atheism worse than Polytheism?........... 104

Chapter Second.

Of the proofs of the existence of God..................... 105
    Article First.—Metaphysical argument............... 105
    Article Second.—Physical argument....... 109
    Article Third.—Moral argument..................... 112

PART SECOND.—THE ATTRIBUTES OF GOD.

Chapter First.

Of the unity of God................................... 116
    Article First.—The unity of God proved against the Polytheists.................................. 116
    Article Second—The unity of God against the Dualists 118
    Article Third.—The origin of evil under a being infinitely good 119

Chapter Second.

Of the eternity of God..... 121

Chapter Third.

Of the immutability of God.... 122

Chapter Fourth.

Of the liberty of God.................................. 122
    Article First.—The existence of the liberty of God.... 123
    Article Second.—Pantheism......... 124
    Article Third.—Optimism............................ 126

Chapter Fifth.

Of the omnipotence and independence of God............ 128

Chapter Sixth.

Of the simplicity of God.. 129

Chapter Seventh.

Of the immensity of God 130

Chapter Eighth.

Of the knowledge of God.................................... 131

Chapter Ninth.

Of the wisdom of God 133

Chapter Tenth.

Of the sanctity and veracity of God........................ 134

Chapter Eleventh.

Of the goodness and happiness of God...................... 134

Chapter Twelfth.

Of the justice of God..................................... 135

Chapter Thirteenth.

Of the providence of God.................................. 135
    Article First.—The existence of providence............ 135
    Article Second.—Consequences of the existence of providence in regard to the free actions of men............ 137

THIRD DISSERTATION.—ON PSYCHOLOGY.

PART FIRST.—EXPERIMENTAL PSYCHOLOGY.

Chapter First.

Of sensibility 141
  (A) Physical sensibility 142
    (a) Organic impressions............................ 142
    (b) Sensations..................................... 143
    (c) Appetite 143
  (B) Interior sensibility................................ 144
    (a) Personal affections 144
    (b) Social desires................................. 145
    (c) Sentiments involving some conception of pure reason.. 145

Chapter Second.

Of the intellect.. 146
   Article First.—The perceptive faculties............... 146
      (A) Experimental perceptions 146
      (B) Rational perceptions, or pure reason............ 147
   Article Second.—The reflective faculties—Language... 148
      (a) General notions................................ 148
      (b) Language considered in relation to thought...... 149
      (c) Origin of language............................. 150
      1st. The question of fact......................... 150
      2nd. The question of possibility 151
   Article Third.—The nature and origin of our ideas ... 152
      1st. The nature of our ideas 152
      2nd. The origin of our ideas...................... 153
      (a) System of the Sensists........................ 154
      (b) The doctrine of innate ideas................... 155
      (c) The doctrine of the intuition of God............ 156

Chapter Third.

Of activity 157
The freedom of the human soul........................... 158

PART SECOND.—RATIONAL PSYCHOLOGY.

Chapter First.

Of the nature of the human soul, or of its spirituality...... 161

Chapter Second.

Of the union of the soul with the body.................... 164

Chapter Third.

Of the destiny of the soul................................. 169

Chapter Fourth.

Of the souls of animals 170
   Article First.—The faculties of the souls of animals.... 170
   Article Second.—The nature and destiny of the souls of animals... 172

PART THIRD.—ETHICS; OR, MORAL PHILOSOPHY.

FIRST DISSERTATION.—ON HUMAN ACTIONS IN GENERAL.

Chapter First.

Of the difference between good and bad actions 178
    Article First.—The difference between moral good and moral evil............................. 179
    Article Second—The obligations of doing good and avoiding evil, or the existence of the natural law.... 181
    Article Third.—The promulgation of this natural law.. 184
    Article Fourth.—The immutability of the natural law.. 186
    Article Fifth.—The sanction of the natural law........ 187

Chapter Second.

Of the principles of good and bad actions................. 190

Chapter Third.

Rules for distinguishing good from bad actions............ 191

SECOND DISSERTATION.—ON HUMAN ACTIONS IN PARTICULAR.

Chapter First.

Of the duties of men towards God 193
    Article First.—The necessity of religious worship..... 193
    Article Second.—The causes which induce men either to neglect or to corrupt the worship of God 197

Chapter Second.

Of the duties of man towards himself................... 197
    Article First.—The obligation of preserving the life of the body................. 198

Article Second.—The obligation of cultivating the faculties of the mind 203
   (a) The culture of the intellect.................... 203
   (b) The culture of the sensibility................. 207
   (c) The culture of the will....................... 208

Chapter Third.

Duties of man towards his fellow men 209
  (A) Destiny of man for the state of society.......... 209
  (B) Consequences resulting from the state of society: Inequality of conditions in life—right of property.... 211

DUTIES OF MEN IN THEIR RELATIONS WITH SOCIETY.

Article First.—Duties of men in relation to domestic society 215
   (a) Conjugal society 215
   (b) Parental society............................. 216
   (c) *Herile* society 216
Article Second.—The duties of men in relation to civil society 216
I. Civil society considered in itself 217
  (A) Nature of civil society and its various forms.... 217
  (B) The supreme power in civil society............ 218
    (a) Characteristics and attributes of the supreme power.. 218
    (b) Origin and foundation of the supreme power 218
    (c) Means by which it is acquired.............. 219
    (d) Causes for which supreme power may be taken from a ruler.. 221
II. Duties of men considered as members of civil society 222
Article Third.—Duties of men towards one another.... 223
  I. Positive duties..................................... 223
  II. Negative duties—Duels........................... 223